Animals in Origami

Acknowledgments
I should like to thank Nina and Angelo, Olivier Ploton, the photographer, and all the editorial team.

A DAVID & CHARLES BOOK
© Dessain et Tolra/Larousse 2010

Originally published in France as *Zoorigami*
First published in the UK and USA in 2012 by F&W Media International, Ltd.

David & Charles is an imprint of F&W Media International, Ltd
Brunel House, Forde Close, Newton Abbot, TQ12 4PU, UK

F&W Media International, Ltd is a subsidiary of F+W Media, Inc
10151 Carver Road, Cincinnati OH45242, USA

ISBN-13: 978-1-4463-0231-6 paperback
ISBN-10: 1-4463-0231-8 paperback

Printed in China by RR Donnelley
for David & Charles
Brunel House Newton Abbot Devon

Photography credits:
p 16, p 121, p 123, © Josef F Stuefer - Fotolia.com; p 16, p 125, p 127 © Ibizarre - Fotolia.com; p 18, p 129, p 131 © Marc Azema - Fotolia.com; p 20, p 133, p 135 © Alex Romantsov - Fotolia.com; p 23, p 137, p 139 © Parkhomenko Andrey - Fotolia.com; p 26, p 141, p 143 © Bukda - Fotolia.com; p 28, p 145, p 147 © Eleden - Fotolia.com; p 30, © Vinicius Tupinamba - Fotolia.com; p 30, p 149, p 151 © Marjory Duc - Fotolia.com; p 32, p 153, p 155 © Odina - Fotolia.com; p 34, p 157, p 159 © Bohi - Fotolia.com; p 36, p 161, p 163 Aleksandra Kosev - Fotolia.com; p 40, p 165, p 167 © Bonniemarie - Fotolia.com; p 43, p 169, p 171 © katsu - Fotolia.com; p 46, p 173, p 175 © Lena Rozova - Fotolia.com; p 50, p 177, p 179 © Vitaly Pakhnyushchyy - Fotolia.com; p 52, p 181, p 183 © Beltsazar - Fotolia.com; p 54, p 185, p 187 © Sergii Shalimov - Fotolia.com; p 56 © Joss - Fotolia.com p 56, p 189, p 191 © Claudio Baldini - Fotolia.com; p 58, p 193, p 195 © Olga Lis - Fotolia.com; p 60, p 197, p 199 © Alena Yakusheva - Fotolia.com; p 64, p 201, p 203 © Maximilian Effgen - Fotolia.com; p 65 © Lisa F. Young - Fotolia.com; p 67, p 205, p 207 © Alri - Fotolia.com; p 70, p 209, p 211 © kim - Fotolia.com; p 72, p 213, p 215, © Eco View - Fotolia.com; p 72, p 217, p 219 © Marilyn Barbone - Fotolia.com; p 75, p 221, p 223 © Eline Spek - Fotolia.com; p 78, p 225, p 227 © Roman Sigaev - Fotolia.com; p 80 © Suprijono Suharjoto - Fotolia.com; p 80, p 229, p 231 © Robby Schenk - Fotolia.com; p 82 © Aussiebloke - Fotolia.com; p 82, p 233, p 235 © Martin 1985 - Fotolia.com; p 86, p 237, p 239 © Adam Borkowski; p 88, p 241, p 243 © Laure Fons - Fotolia.com; p 90, p 245, p 247 © PsamtiK - Fotolia.com; p 94, p 249, p 251, p 253, p 255 © Xygo_bg - Fotolia.com; p 94, p 257, p 259, p 261, p 263 © Bonsy - Fotolia.com; p 98, p 265, p 267 © Gina Smith - Fotolia.com; p 98, p 102, p 269, p 271, p 273, p 275 © Sergii Shalimov- Fotolia.com; p 102, p 277, p 279 © Roman Sigaev - Fotolia.com; p 106, p 281, p 283 © Anette Linnea Rasmussen - Fotolia.com; p 106, p 285, p 287 © Marilyn Barbone - Fotolia.com; p 106, p 289, p 291 © Joss - Fotolia.com; p 106, p 293, p 295 © Felinda - Fotolia.com; p 106, p 297, p 299 © ReSeandra - Fotolia.com; p 106, p 301, p 303 © Alri - Fotolia.com; p 106, p 305, p 307 © Kiol-picture - Fotolia.com; p 106, p 309, p 311 © Handmade - Fotolia.com; p 106, p 313, p 315 © Lefebvre Jonathan - Fotolia.com; p 106, p 317, p 319 © Geofff - Fotolia.com; p 106, p 321, p 323 © Jim Parkin - Fotolia.com; p 106, p 325, p 327 © Freesurf - Fotolia.com; p 106, p 329, p 331 © German Cheung - Fotolia.com; p 106, p 333, © Christopher Ursitti - Fotolia.com; p 106, p 335 © Anette Linnea Rasmussen - Fotolia.com; p 106, p 337 © Beatuerkn - Fotolia.com; p 106, p 339 © Azat Ayupov - Fotolia.com; p 106, p 341 © Dacuks - Fotolia.com.

Editorial board and editorial coordination: Colette Hanicotte
Editing: Corinne de Montalembert with the help of Natalia Dobiecka
Proofing: Madeleine Biaujeaud
Graphic design and layout: Either
Cover: Véronique Laporte
Photography Olivier Ploton
Photogravure: IGS-CP Angoulême
Model making: Anne Raynaud

F+W Media publishes high quality books on a wide range of subjects.
For more great book ideas visit: **www.rucraft.co.uk**

Foreword

Nowadays, origami is a universal language, practised all over the world by people of all ages. The increasing attraction for this art form owes itself to creators who have been able to update its traditional themes. Through my observation of nature, I've created these origami animals for you in all their different finery; little contemporary sculptures that are an aesthetic, minimalist and poetic expression.

I will show you how to recreate these zany domestic or wild animals using minimal materials and following simple and precise steps. Each creation is a combination of my imagination and the characteristic expression of the animal. Some of the little mascots are like cartoon creatures: unlikely collections that are both amazing and humourous. Have fun making your own amusing mascots by experimenting with the different heads and bodies.

Origami is an ephemeral art that invites you to reflect and to stay zen. I hope that these models will make us all aware that some species of animal are under threat of extinction due to the damage caused to their environment and the many types of pollution.

I hope that you will get a lot of enjoyment from folding these origami animals.

Didier Boursin

Contents

Savannahs, deserts and oceans...

Farm favourites...

Folds and symbols
> Advice

Before starting, take a look at the 'Folds and symbols' (see pp. 6–9) and 'Diagrams of the bases and details' pages (see pp. 10–13), which explain the essential folds. These include the 'valley' fold (crease is at the bottom) and the 'mountain' fold (crease is at the top), as well as other movements and combinations of folds that will subsequently be useful.

Each fold and its movement are represented in a diagram by an arrow and dots to be joined together. To avoid making any mistakes make sure you know the difference between 'folding the paper' and 'marking the crease'. In the first instance, you make the fold; in the second, you crease it as indicated by the double arrow. If necessary, refer to the subsequent diagram which will also help you understand the previous step.

At first, you should practise folding simple models in a square format using ordinary paper. The best papers are those that are no more than 90g (3¼in), such as Pop'Set or Kraft. Then, move on to making the animals in the recommended papers suggested at the end of the book (see pp. 120–344) or in any other paper of your choice. You'll find that the random fall of the folds makes the object look different each time.

We have marked the level of difficulty of the folds using shaded diamonds. Start out by folding easy models so that you can learn the basic terminology, acquire a light touch and achieve accuracy with your movements. Some people aren't immediately successful at paper folding, but don't let that put you off. Your second attempt will often be better than your first. For each origami model, you have two chances at succeeding with your paper folding, or in any case, enough paper to make two examples.

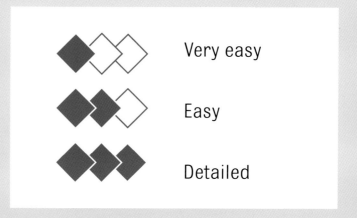

Very easy

Easy

Detailed

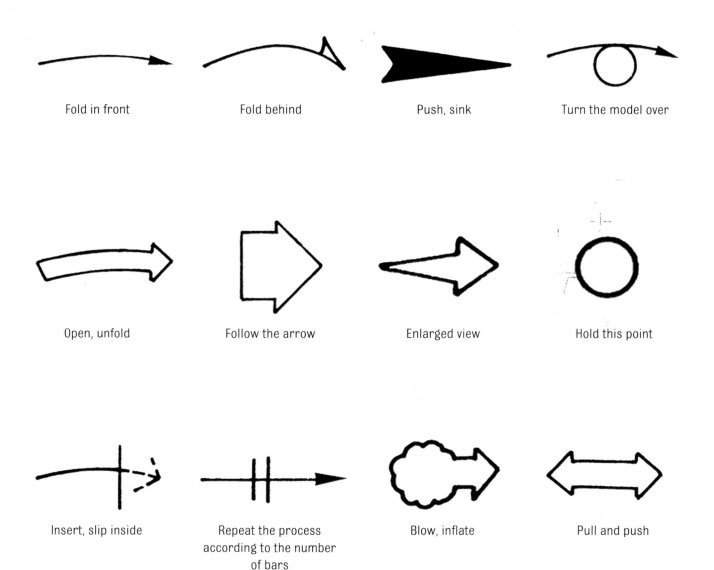

Fold in front

Fold behind

Push, sink

Turn the model over

Open, unfold

Follow the arrow

Enlarged view

Hold this point

Insert, slip inside

Repeat the process
according to the number
of bars

Blow, inflate

Pull and push

Folds and symbols

> Main folds

> Valley fold

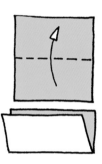

> Mountain fold

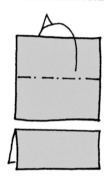

> Mark the crease

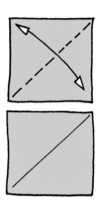

> Pleat fold

> Join up the dots

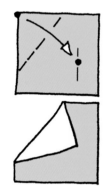

> Cut

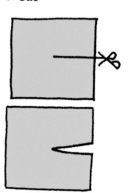

> Inside reverse fold

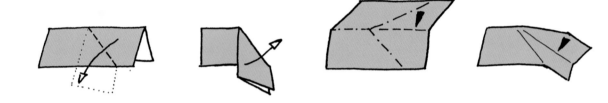

> Outside reverse fold

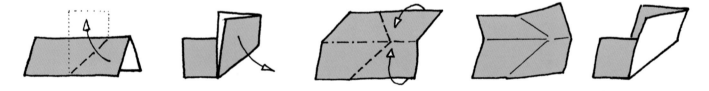

Diagrams of the bases and details

> Preliminary base

   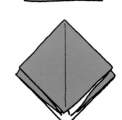

By pressing with your finger at the centre (a), you can obtain the water bomb base below.

 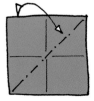 

> Water bomb base

By pressing with your finger at the centre (b), you can obtain the preliminary base above.

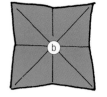  

> Bird base

  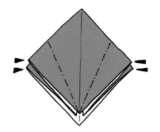

1. Fold the bottom edges onto the centre crease on both faces using a preliminary base (see p. 10).

2. Unfold.

3. Push the sides in using inside reverse folds (see p. 9).

> Bird's legs

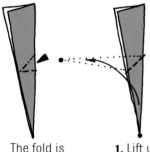   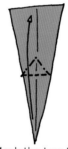

The fold is performed in two stages:

1. Lift up the tip horizontally.

2. Fold over to the right.

3. Unfold completely.

4. Mark the two top sides of the triangle using mountain fold (see p. 8), then lift up the tip using valley fold (see p. 8) along the remaining side of the triangle.

5. Fold in half by placing the sides of the triangle in mountain fold.

Diagrams of the bases and details

> Fish beak

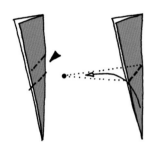 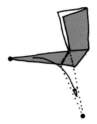   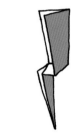

1. Lift up the tip horizontally.

2. Fold the tip back downwards. To make a beak, fold the tip more to the right, keeping it parallel.

3. Unfold completely.

4. Mark the mountain and valley folds (see p. 8) as indicated, then fold in half along the vertical fold.

5. Fold flat.

> Fish base

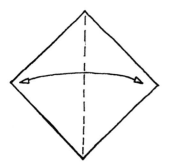

1. Mark the vertical crease.

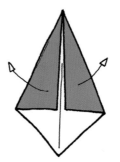

2. Fold the upper edges onto the centre crease.

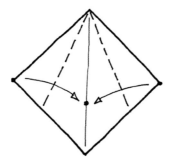

3. Unfold.

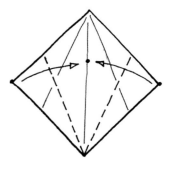

4. Fold the lower edges in the same way.

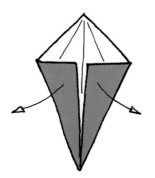

5. Unfold.

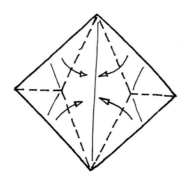

6. Fold over the edges whilst pinching the side points at the same time.

7. Flatten, placing the points upwards.

Savannahs, deserts and oceans...

Arabian horse

In some countries, the horse is the most reliable form of transport. For us, it's usually a good walking or riding companion.

For recommended paper, see pp. 121–128.

1. **Mark the creases** then make the preliminary base (see p. 10).

2. **Fold** the sides, joining up the dots on the two faces.

3. **Cut** through a single thickness on each of the two faces then unfold the sides.

4. **Lift up** the tips, as indicated, on the two faces.

5. **Fold** in half, as indicated, on the two faces.

6. **Tip** the fold upside down.

7. **Mark the creases** along the dotted lines, then make reverse folds (see p. 9) to form the head and the tail.

8. **Fold back** the tip of the head.

To make the horse flip over completely and land back on his feet, lift him up quickly using a finger.

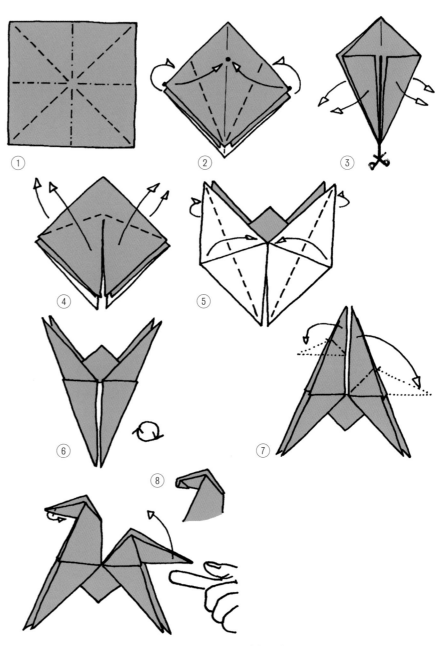

arabian horse > 17

Desert lizard

The desert lizard likes to hide from the sun in cool, shady areas, making it unlikely to be spotted. However, this striking decorative lizard is sure to catch your eye.

For recommended paper, see pp. 129–132.

Perform steps 1, 2 and 3 of the Desert fox cub (see p. 21).

1 **Unfold** completely.

2 **Refold**, keeping to the direction of the creases.

3 **Flatten**, slipping the sides underneath.

4 **Fold over** the tips as indicated, then turn over.

5 **Fold over** to the centre crease, folding the underneath triangle in half as on the left side.

6 **Cut** along the line on each side then turn over.

7 **Fold over** the edges. To make the hind legs appear, fold the tips towards the outside. Fold the forelegs like the one on the left. To make the head, make a bird base (see p. 11).

8 **Make** the other hind leg then fold over the tips and turn over.

9 **Give** the body some volume by folding it in half then raising the legs. To make the head, crease the triangle and fold over behind the tip.

Detail for the head

9a **Give** the head some volume along the creases indicated.

9b **Check** the finished head is as shown.

Bend the lizard into a zigzag shape:

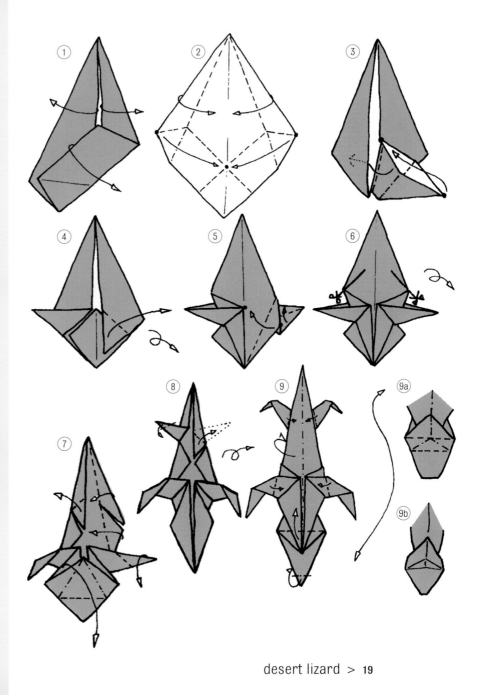

desert lizard > **19**

Desert fox cub

In summer as in winter, the fox will be wearing his fur coat. In the desert, he spends all day sleeping down a nice, cool hole and only emerges at night to prowl.

For recommended paper, see pp. 133–136.

1 **Fold down** the sides onto the centre crease.

2 **Mark** the creases, joining up the dots.

3 **Unfold.**

4 **Open** the sides along the creased folds.

5 **Fold** the tips in half and flatten the bottom triangle.

Detail

5a **Open** as for the bird base (see p. 11).

6 **Fold** the two legs as on the left then fold in half.

7 **Lift** up the front part in a reverse fold (see p. 9).

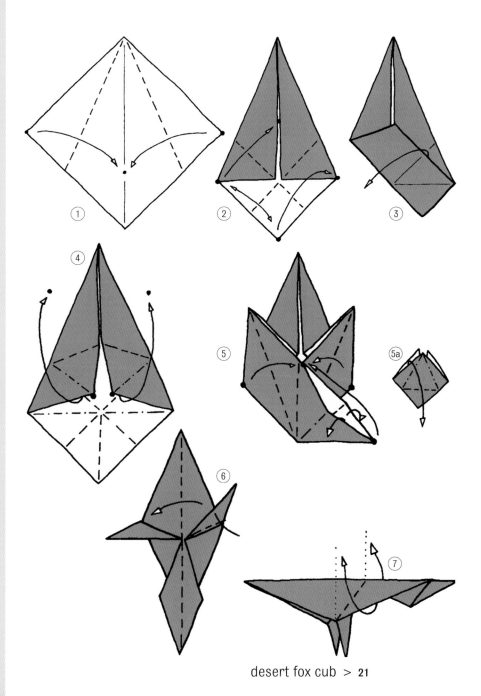

desert fox cub > 21

Desert fox cub

(cont.)

8 **Make** a cut along the bold line then make a pleat fold to tilt the head forwards.

9 **Fold over** the angular part. Roll up the tip of the muzzle. Cut at the back along the bold line then make a pleat fold to form the legs.

10 **Turn in** the triangles at the ears.

11 **Make** a pleat fold (see p. 8) to lower the tail towards the rear.

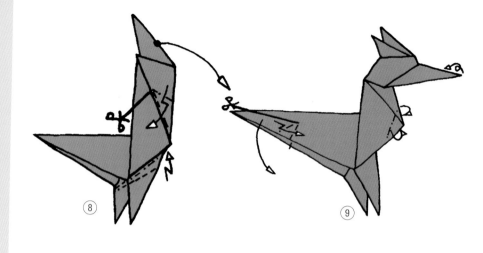

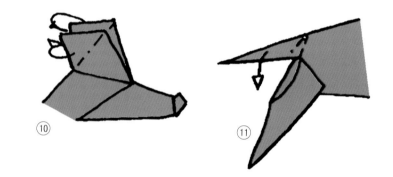

Warthog

This solitary animal has a large head and two useful tusks that are used for digging and as a defence against predators.

For recommended paper, see pp. 137–140.

Warthog (cont.)

1 **Fold down** the sides onto the centre crease.

2 **Check** your model is as shown then turn over.

3 **Fold** in half, joining up the dots.

4 **Fold** the sides, drawing down the centre part (see fish base, p. 13).

5 **Fold** in the two tips.

6 **Draw down** the rear tip.

7 **Fold** in half.

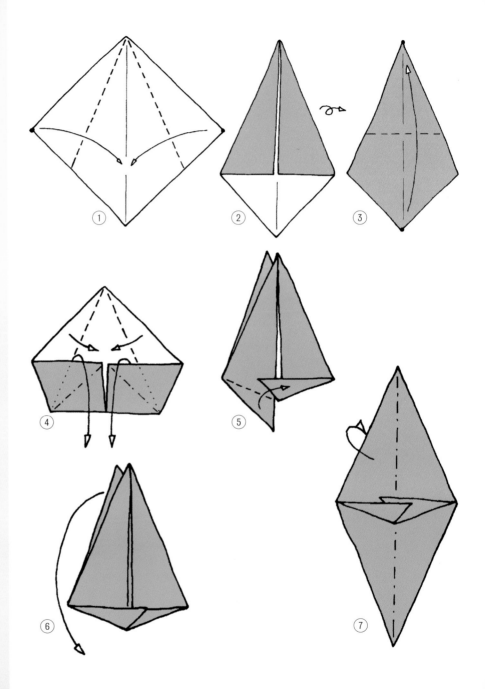

8 **Make** a pleat fold (see p. 8) on each side.

9 **Make** a reverse fold (see p. 9) in the front then make a pleat fold as indicated.

Detail for the head

9a **Lift up** the tip.

9b **Fold over** the tip and fold the angular part.

9c **Fold** the ears and fold the muzzle. Mark the crease at the rear then make a reverse fold by opening the fold.

Detail for the rear

10 **Make** a pre-crease then make a reverse fold.

11 **Push** the triangle into the reverse fold.

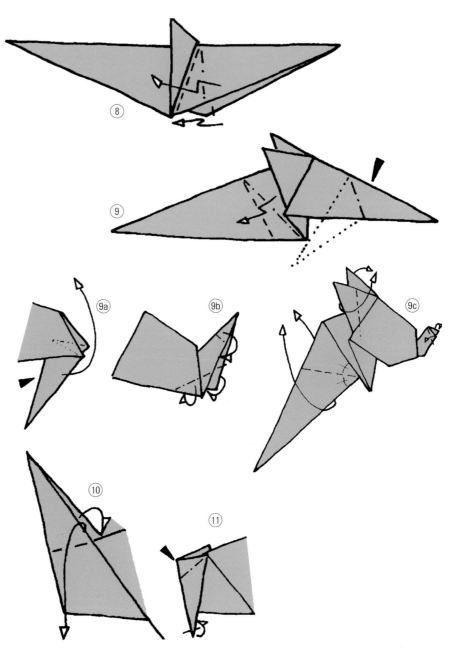

Elephant calf

In Asia, the elephant is a symbol of wisdom. These pretty pink calves dressed in oriental paper remind us that an elephant never forgets.

For recommended paper, see pp. 141–145.

1 **Start** with the fish base (see p. 13) and mark the crease, joining up the dots.

2 **Make** a cut (black line) then fold the tip at the bottom by pinching it to push it into this cut.

3 **Fold** in half, keeping to the creases indicated.

4 **Make** a reverse fold (see p. 9) using the dotted line as a guideline. Make a pleat fold in the two forelegs.

5 **Fold over** the angular parts inside. Fold over the end of the forelegs.

6 **Form** the head by tilting the tip forward to make a pleat fold (see p. 8) on the two faces. Fold back the tail downwards using a pleat fold on each side.

7 **Form** the trunk by making a pleat fold then folding over the end.

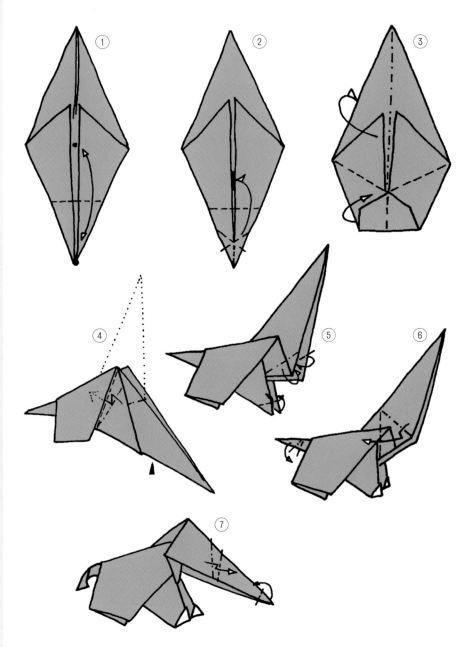

Monkey

This funny little marmoset likes to do acrobatics and pull faces. He's very cheeky and is happy to perform his tricks in return for payment in peanuts!

For recommended paper, see pp. 145–148.

1. **Fold** a fish base (see p .13) and fold in half. Fold the sides into the centre, pulling out flat as on the left.

2. **Lift up** the legs and fold as indicated then turn back the tail downwards.

3. **Fold over** the other leg and fold everything in half.

4. **Lift up** the tail, making a reverse fold (see p. 9). To form the head, draw down the tip, opening it out.

5. **Finish off** the tail by making several reverse folds as indicated.

6. **Form** the ears by making a pleat fold (see p. 8) in the reverse folds then make another pleat fold, as indicated. To form the nose, open the tip and flatten.

7. **Finish** by making a pleat fold to give volume to the muzzle.

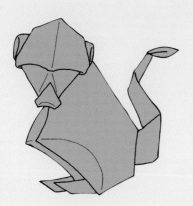

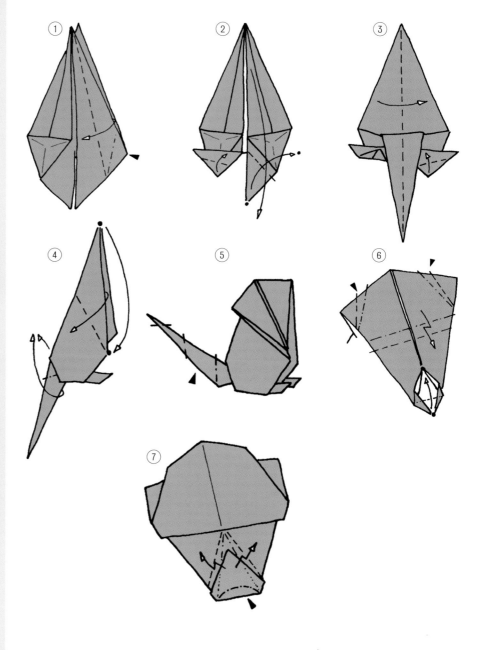

Bear

During the cold weather, the bear hibernates in his lair, reappearing in the spring. His highly developed sense of smell enables him to find his favourite dessert: honey from the hives.

For recommended paper, see pp. 149–152.

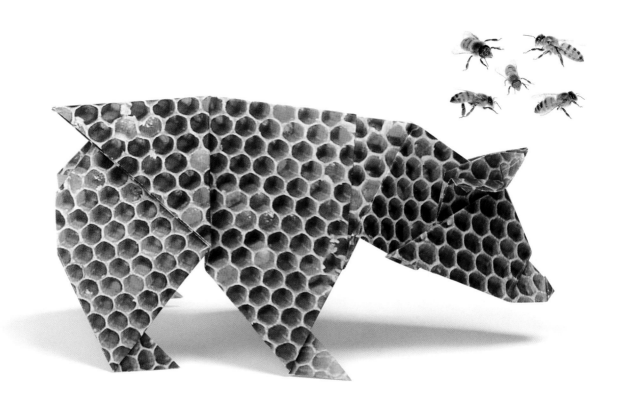

To make the bear, you need two squares of paper. Fold steps 1 to 5 of the pig (see p. 44).

1 **Fold** in half.

2 **Form** the ears by opening the tips and flattening them. In the centre, make a pleat fold (see p. 8) on each side. Make a reverse fold (see p. 9) so that the tail appears then fold the legs as indicated.

Detail for the ear

2a **Fold** the tip, then the edges, then fold in half.

3 **Make** a pleat fold at the level of the ears, then make a pleat fold at the head and fold over the tip of the muzzle.

4 **Fold** the angular part behind then make a pleat fold to lower the head. Open the top swiftly with your finger to make the ears appear.

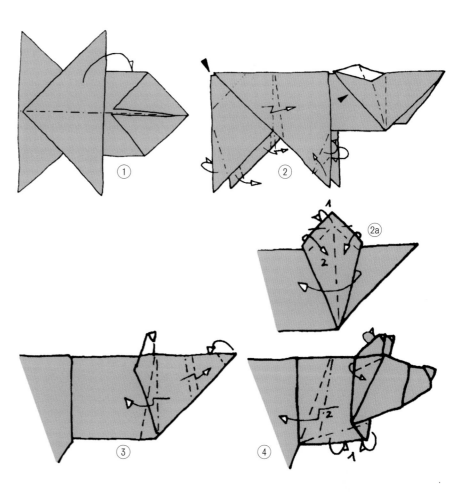

Whale

The whale is one of the largest marine mammals, yet despite its size, it is one of the most elegant and graceful of the ocean dwellers.

For recommended paper, see pp. 153–156.

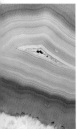

1 **Fold down** the sides.

2 **Fold over** the two other sides.

3 **Fold** down in half.

4 **Fold** in half.

5 **Make** a reverse fold at the rear after pre-creasing (see p. 9).

6 **Lift up** one tip in a reverse fold.

Detail for folding the tip of the tail

7 **Make** two reverse folds to finish the tail. Cut out a thin strip to represent the jet of water. Turn over.

8 **Bend** into a cylinder, then fit the sides into each other.

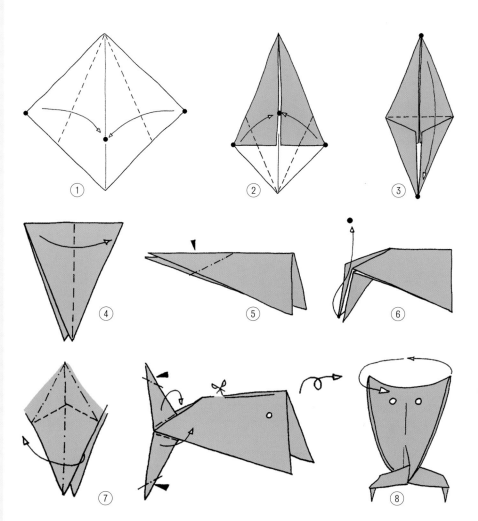

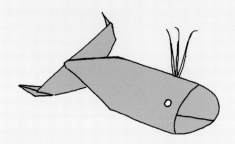

Little fish

Little fish live together in shoals. They like the open sea where they can surf the waves.

For recommended paper, see pp. 157–160.

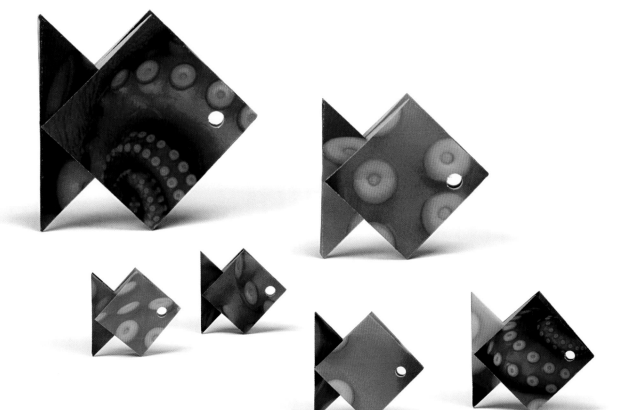

To make a little fish, you will need two small 9cm (3½in) squares of paper.

Detail for the body

1 **Mark** the creases as indicated.

2 **Fold** everything together, joining up the dots.

3 **Check** the finished body is as shown.

Detail for the tail

1 **Make** the same folds as for the body, then unfold.

2 **Fold** the two sides into the centre.

3 **Mark** the creases on the other two sides.

4 **Fold** everything together as in step 1.

5 **Push** the rear triangle inside, combining all the thicknesses.

6 **Push** the front triangle inside in the same way.

7 **The fold** has two pockets for the assembly, as shown.

Assembling the body and tail

1 **Slip** the inner tips of the body into the pockets of the triangle.

2 **Make** it stand up by slightly parting the tips. Finally, punch a hole in the paper for the eyes.

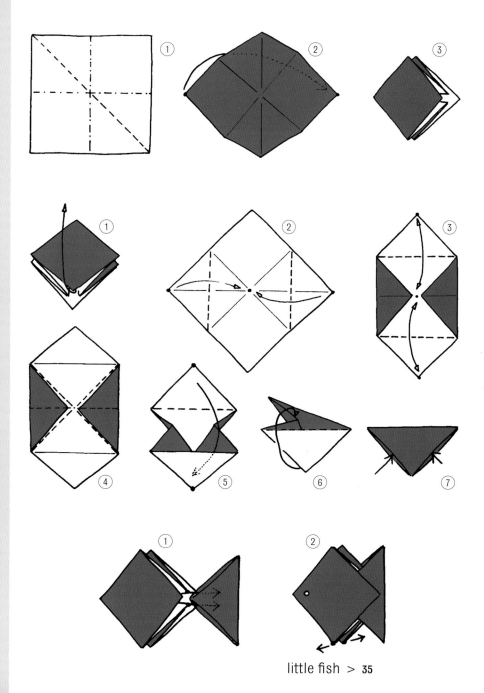

little fish > **35**

Inflatable fish

Some little fish puff themselves out to impress or intimidate the bigger fish that they encounter. This clever little fish can also be inflated by simply blowing into it.

For recommended paper, see pp. 161–164.

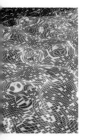

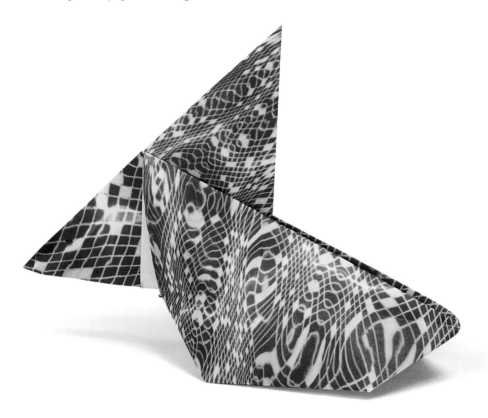

1. **Make** a water bomb base (see p. 10) then lift up the top tips.
2. **Fold down** the sides toward the centre.
3. **Fold** the two tips to the centre.
4. **Slip** the triangles into the pockets.
5. **Check** your model is as shown, then turn over.
6. **Fold** the sides towards the centre.
7. **Lift** the tip into a horizontal position.
8. **Fold** the right part towards the left.
9. **Give** the fish volume by blowing air into it to inflate it.

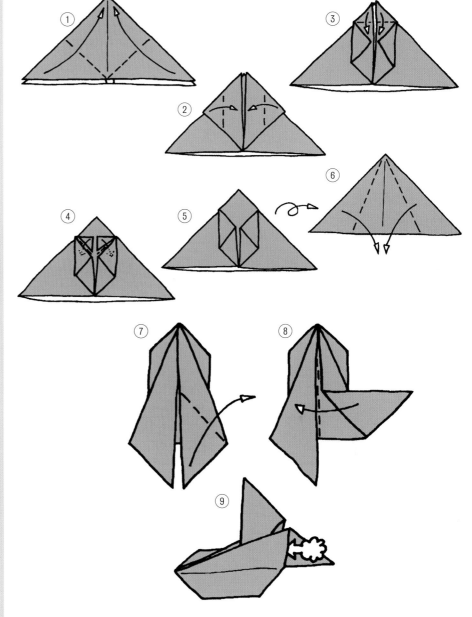

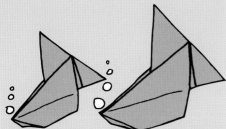

Farm favourites...

Goose

With its head down, the goose squawks, hisses, cackles and clucks among its friends in the courtyard.

For recommended paper, see pp. 165–168.

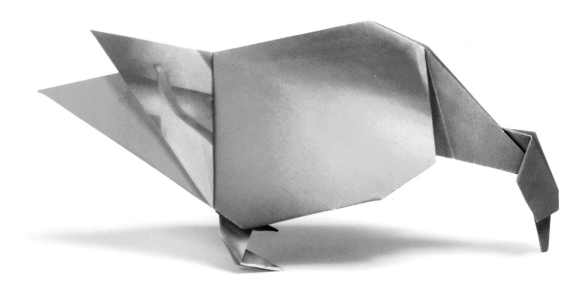

1. **Fold down** the sides.
2. **Fold** the bottom triangle to the back.
3. **Mark** the creases as indicated.
4. **Make** two reverse folds (see p. 9) as on the left then fold down the tips towards the outside. Reduce the tips by folding them in half then turn over.
5. **Fold back** the square then fold in half.
6. **Fold back** the angular parts.
7. **Make** a reverse fold for the head.

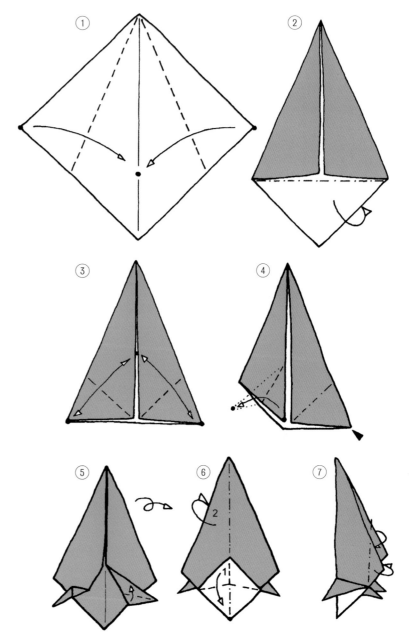

goose > 41

Goose (cont.)

Detail for the head

7a **Mark** the creases.

7b **Fold over**, pushing a part inside.

7c **Lift up** the tip in a reverse fold.

7d **Make** a pleat fold (see p. 8) to tilt the tip.

7e **Make** the beak by using a pleat fold then fold the tip as indicated.

7f **Fold over** the extending part.

Detail for the legs

8 **Make** a pleat fold to flatten the webbed feet.

9 **Check** your model is as shown.

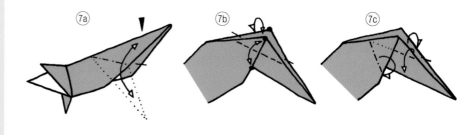

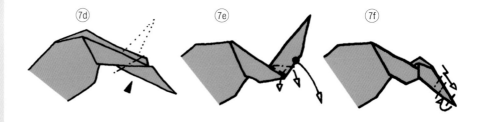

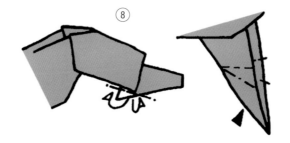

Pig

Sometimes the pig dreams of taking a lovely, scented bath. His floral outfit is a work of art, making him a pretty little pig.

For recommended paper, see pp. 169–172.

Pig (cont.)

1 **Make** this fold by using two squares of paper. With the first square, make a water bomb base (see p. 10) then fold the second layer of paper onto the tip.

2 **Open** then flatten.

3 **Check** your model as shown then turn over.

4 **Fold** the sides of the second square onto the centre crease.

5 **Fold over** the four corners then unfold the right side and open, folding over the front. Fit the two parts together.

6 **Fold** the tip to the right then give it volume by folding in half.

7 **Make** the tail by make a pleat fold (see p. 8) using a reverse fold (see p. 9). Fold the legs as indicated. Next, fold the ears downwards. To form the head, make a pleat fold using a reverse fold. Make a pleat fold in the centre as indicated.

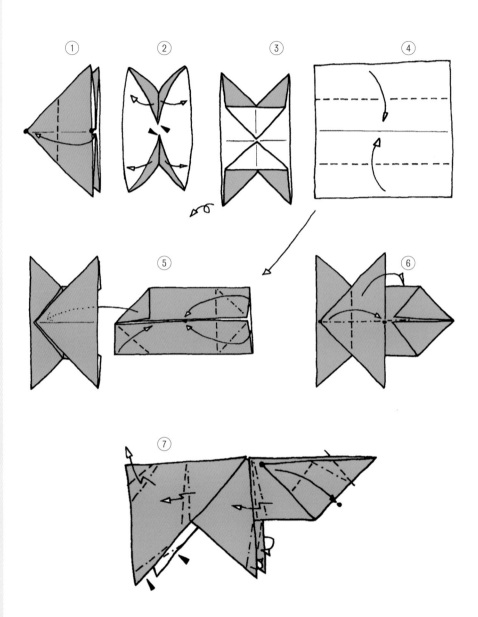

Details

7a **Make** the tail.

7b **Make** the hind legs by inverting the tip.

7c **Check** the hind legs are as shown.

7d **Make** the forelegs by folding the tips to the front.

7e **Check** the forelegs are as shown.

8 **Fold** over part of the ears.

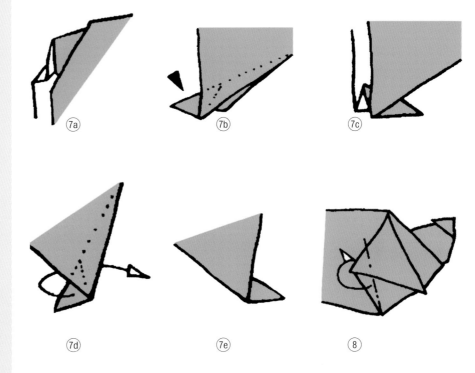

Ram

They say to count sheep when you can't sleep. This little ram with it's peaceful cloud-patterned paper will soon have you on your way to the land of Nod.

For recommended paper, see pp. 173–176.

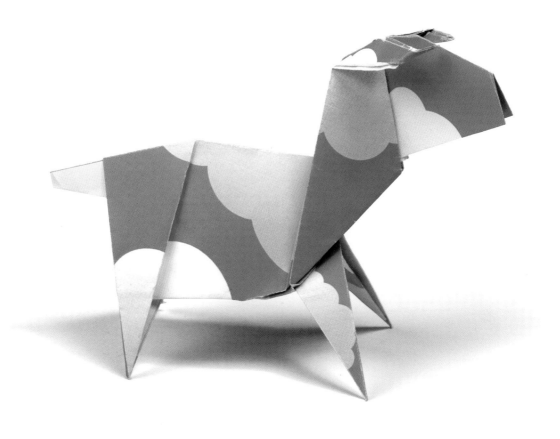

1. **Fold over**, joining up the dots.

2. **Check** your model is as shown, then turn over.

3. **Fold over**, joining up the dots.

4. **Lift up** by opening to the right.

5. **Open** as indicated.

6. **Fold** the sides into the centre.

7. **Fold** in half on each face.

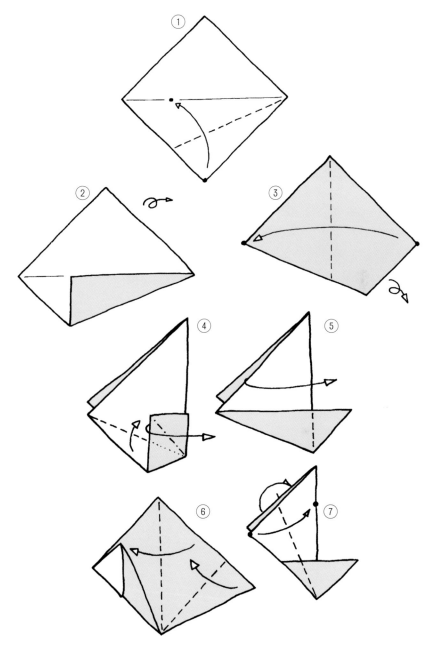

Ram (cont.)

8 **Fold over** the top triangle and make a reverse fold (see p. 9) for the other triangle.

9 **Mark** the crease on the top part and make a reverse fold from the triangle then open out in half.

10 **Form** the legs by opening and flattenning as on the left and lift up the bottom triangle.

11 **Fold** down the tail.

12 **Check** your model is as shown.

13 **Give** it volume folding as indicated.

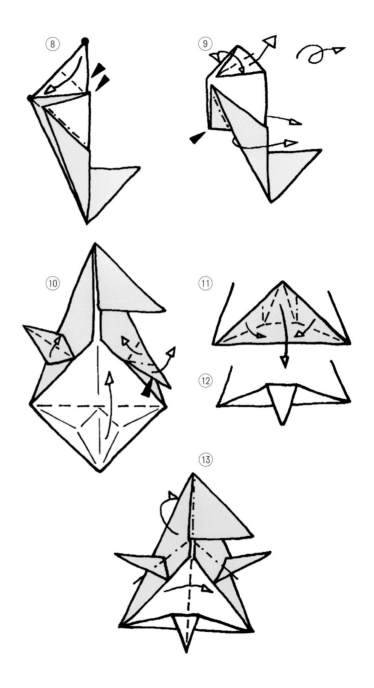

14 **Form** the head by folding the triangle back. To form the legs, make a pleat fold (see p. 8).

Detail for the head

14a **Fold over** to the front.

14b **Pre-crease** as indicated.

14c **Check** your model is as shown, then unfold.

14d **Turn** the folds in the right direction, then slip the pleat fold between the layers.

14e **Form** the horns by cutting the tip, then folding down on each side. Fold the muzzle over.

15 **Finish off** the body by folding the part indicated inside.

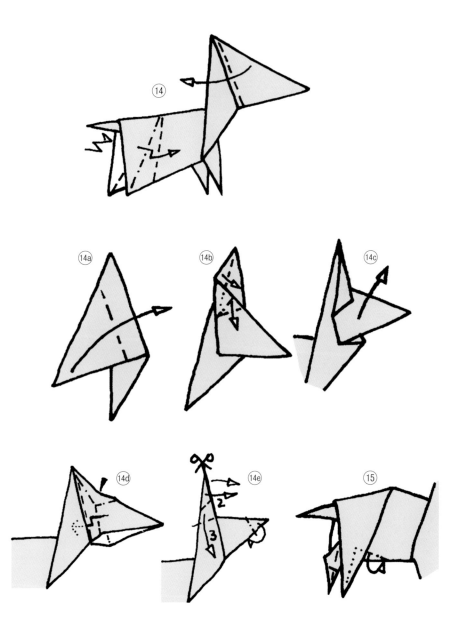

Duck

When a duck has the plumage of a mallard, he's a majestic bird indeed. These ducks are really standing proud.

For recommended paper, see pp. 177–180.

1 **Fold** the fish base (see p. 13), then fold in half.

2 **Make** a reverse fold (see p. 9) on the right tip following the dotted lines.

3 **Fold** the tip in half on each face.

4 **Lift** this tip up in a reverse fold along the dotted lines. Make another reverse fold on the left tip, joining up the dots as indicated.

5 **Fold** the triangle inside on each face on the rear part. To form the head, open the tip, then make a pleat fold (see p. 8) to tilt this tip.

Detail for the head

5a **Make** a pleat fold to form the beak and fold the tip underneath.

5b **Make** a reverse fold in the angular part, then pinch the tip to finish off the beak.

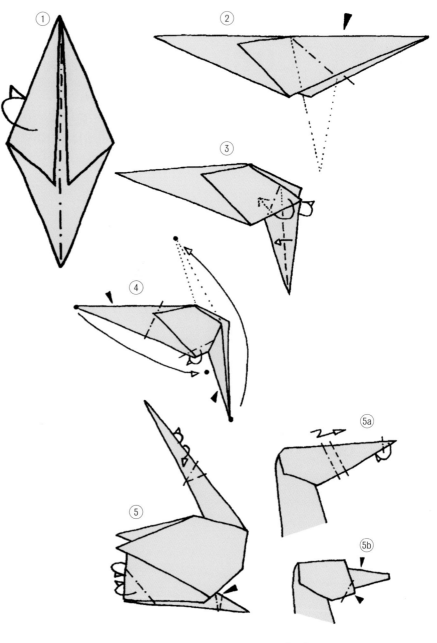

duck > 51

Goat

Goats are known for chewing anything in their path. Don't let one loose in a bookshop, as it'll probably eat all the books on the shelves!

For recommended paper, see pp. 181–184.

1. **Make** a bird base (see p. 11) then turn a sheet to the left on each face.

2. **Give** it volume by folding the tip to the front, folding in half.

3. **Tilt** the forelegs to the front using reverse folds (see p. 9). To form the head, cut the ears in a curve then make a reverse fold to tilt the head forward. To form the hind legs, cut the bold lines then fold the two legs inside.

4. **Fold** the tip of the head, then reduce the neck by folding over inside. Fold the hind legs in half then make a pleat fold in the tail.

Detail for the head

4a **Mark** the crease, drawing down the tip then unfold everything.

4b **Make** a fold to form the beard.

4c **Make** a reverse fold to finish the muzzle.

5. **Fold** the forelegs in half, then make reverse folds in one hind leg and one foreleg.

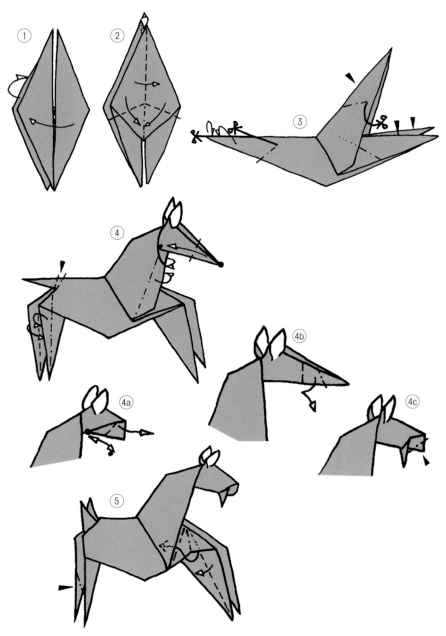

goat > **53**

Guard dog

Who is this dog, with his beautiful furry coat, looking at? He is constantly on watch to protect his master's land.

For recommended paper, see pp. 185–188.

1. **Fold over** the sides towards the centre.

2. **Check** your model is as shown, then turn over.

3. **Fold** towards the centre, letting the part behind come free.

4. **Fold over** the sides as on the left, then fold the bottom part. Next fold everything in half underneath.

5. **Give** it volume by folding the sides, then fold everything in half.

6. **To form** the head, make a pleat fold on each face. To form the hind legs, cut the bold lines then make a pleat fold (see p. 8) on each side.

7. **Fold over** the angular part on the head and fold over the muzzle. For the legs and the tail, make reverse folds (see p. 9).

Detail for the head

7a. **Make** a pleat fold under the nose and a pleat fold to finish the muzzle.

7b. **Fold** the triangle underneath on each side to finish.

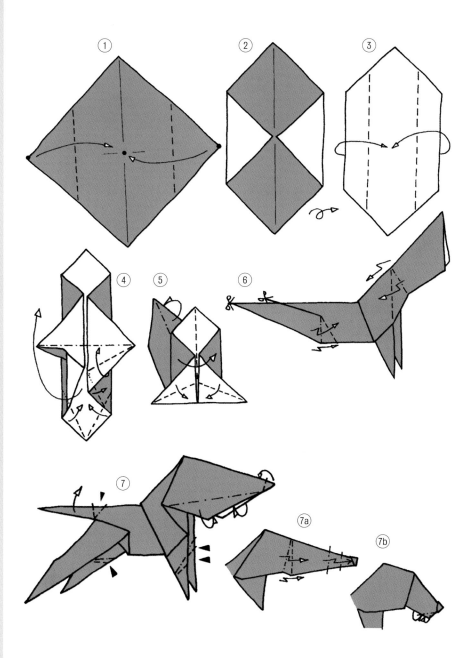

Rabbits

We all know that rabbits love carrots, so keep an eye on him, as he might start munching this paper!

For recommended paper, see pp. 189–192.

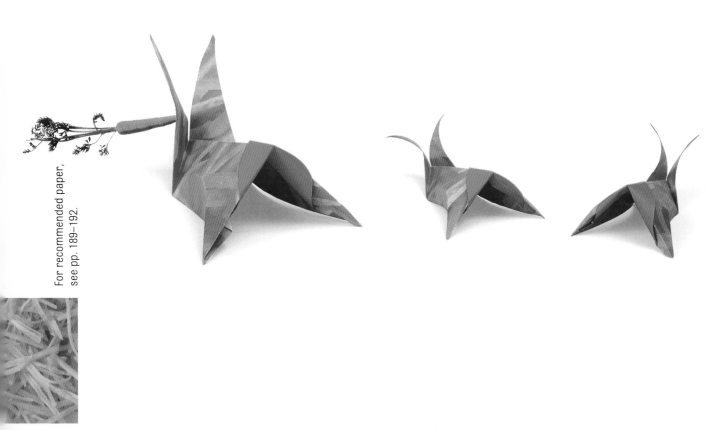

1 **Take** a small square, mark the centre crease and fold the sides along this fold.

2 **Lift up** the triangle and fold it down.

3 **Turn** over and lift the tip to form the tail.

4 **Make** the head by folding the tip downwards.

5 **Fold** in half.

6 **Lift up** the tip of the ears.

7 **Separate** the ears by cutting them.

8 **Give** volume by bending the two sides with your thumbs.

9 **Watch** how these final folds give the impression of movement.

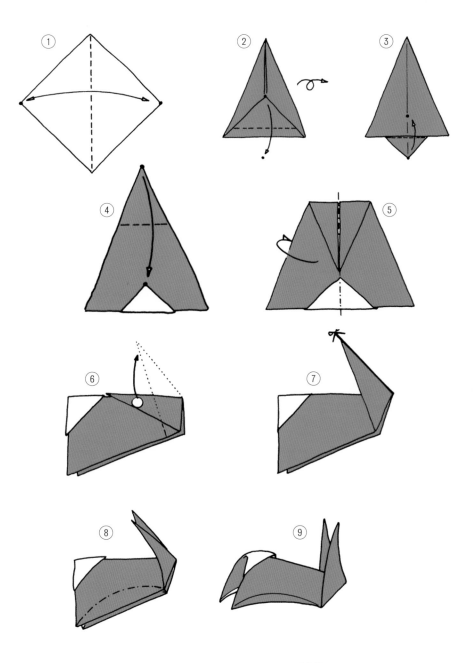

Hare

With its ears pricked, the hare is on alert, ready to bolt for its burrow at the slightest sound.

For recommended paper, see pp. 193–196.

1 **Fold** the sides onto the centre crease.

2 **Fold down** the corners behind as on the left, then bring this section over to the front.

3 **Unfold** towards the centre, holding the dots and lift up the central part.

4 **Fold** the two bottom corners underneath and, with the top part, tilt along the axis indicated.

5 **Fold** the sides, joining up the dots then fold everything in half along the centre crease.

6 **Fold** underneath on each face. At the rear, mark the crease joining up the dots then make a reverse fold (see p. 9).

7 **Make** a pleat fold (see p. 8) for the ears. Fold the tip of the muzzle underneath. For the tail, make a pleat fold. To make the legs, fold inside.

8 **Fold** in half then fold the angular parts inside.

9 **Finish off** the legs by pushing the back part into a reverse fold and making a pleat fold on the two legs.

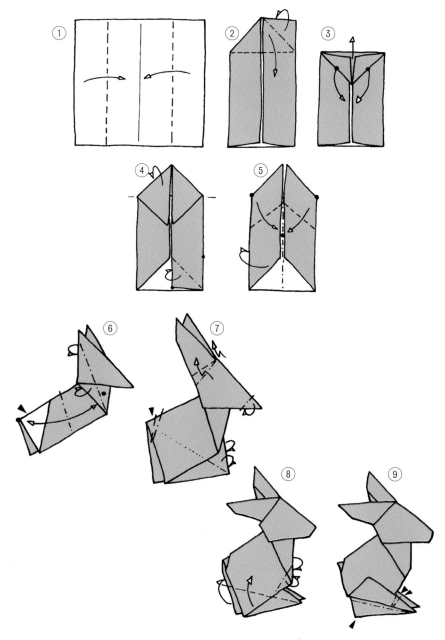

Peacock

The peacock has a distinctive cry and looks quite magnificent when it fans out its colourful tail.

For recommended paper, see pp. 197–200.

1. **Mark** the sides, then fold in half behind.

2. **Mark** the crease in a right angle as indicated, then make a reverse fold (see p. 9) along this crease.

3. **Fold back** the sides to the right.

4. **Divide** each part in half.

5. **Divide** again. To form the head, make a pre-crease then open and flatten.

Detail for the head

5a **Fold** in half.

5b **Make** a pleat fold for the head and another for the beak.

6. **Fold** like an accordion and open out to make the plumage.

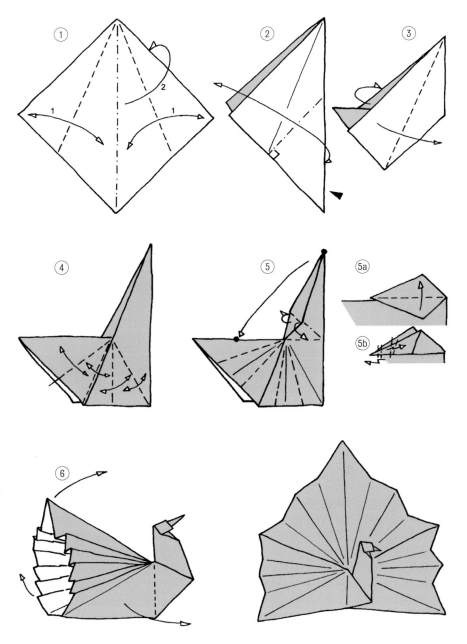

Feathers, fur and scales...

Swan

The swan moves elegantly among the ducks and vegetation at the edge of the water.

For recommended paper, see pp. 201–204.

1. **Fold** in half.

2. **Lift up** the sides.

3. **Fold** as indicated.

4. **Place** the part that is behind on top on both faces.

5. **Open** flat.

6. **Make** a pleat fold.

7. **Fold** in half.

8. **Make** a reverse fold at the front. Make a pleat fold (see p. 8) at the rear using a reverse fold (see p. 9).

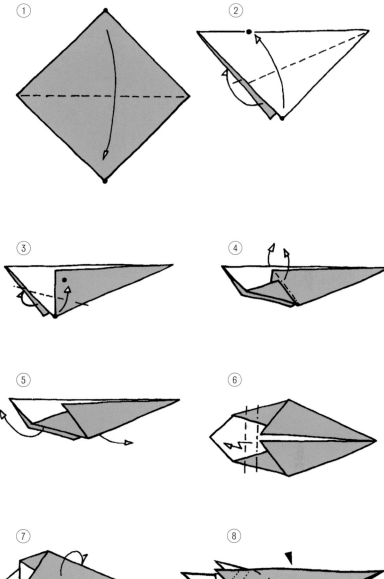

swan > 65

Swan (cont.)

9 **Fold** down the edges at the rear. Fold in half at the front, pushing a part inside.

10 **Lift up** the tip in a reverse fold.

11 **Form** the head by making a reverse fold.

12 **Open** the end then make a pleat fold.

13 **Form** the beak by making a pleat fold using a reverse fold and pushing the tip inside.

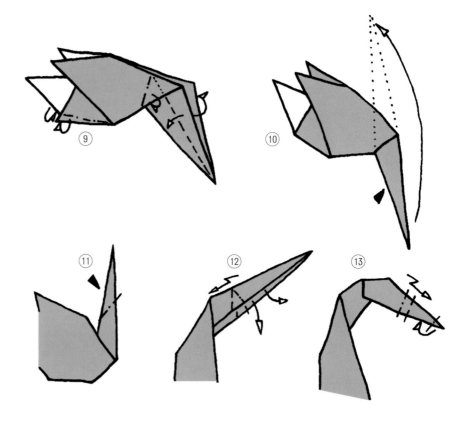

Dragonfly

The dragonfly, like its cousin the damselfly, likes to perform acrobats just above the surface of the water with a bat of its wings.

For recommended paper, see pp. 205–208.

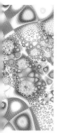

Dragonfly (cont.)

1 **Make** a bird base (see p. 11), then fold one tip downwards.

2 **Lift** the two tips up, open them and flatten them as on the right.

3 **Check** your model is as shown then turn over.

4 **Fold down** the sides along the centre crease, as on the right.

5 **Fold down** the top triangle to the back. Fold the centre strips; the one on the left is folded underneath.

6 **Fold down** the sides towards the centre.

Detail

6a **Fold** by opening the flaps, then unfold the sides.

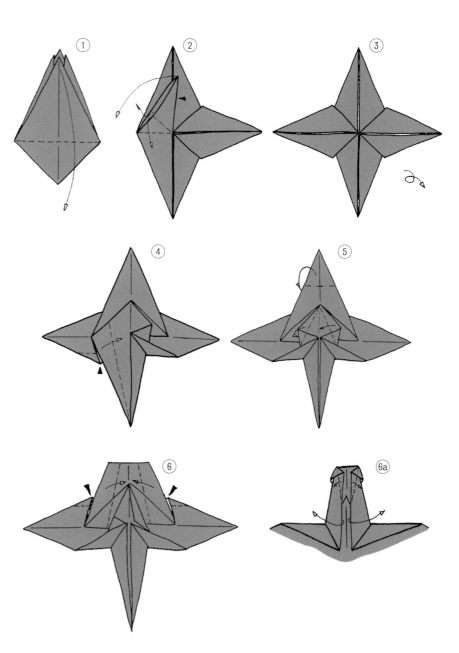

dragonfly > **68**

7 **Fold over** the sides under the central triangle.

8 **Check** your model is as shown, then turn over.

Detail

8a **Fold over** the triangle near the top, then tilt it over to the other side, slipping it under the other thicknesses. Turn over.

9 **Cut** the wings, as indicated, then fold everything in half, wedging the strip on the right under the central triangle.

Detail

9a **Round off** the wings.

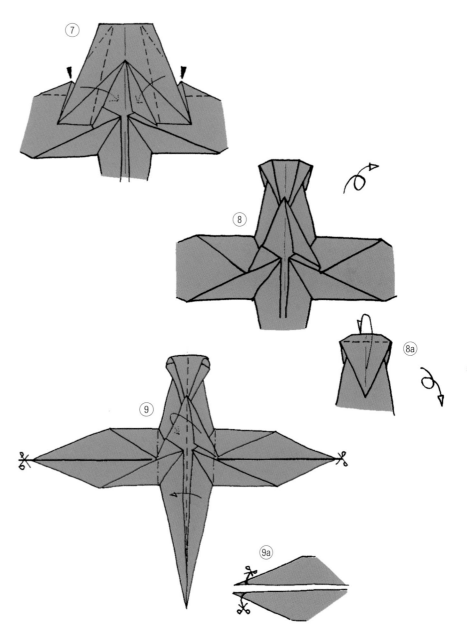

Butterfly

Once you have folded these butterflies, you can imagine them flying away and gracefully landing on your walls.

For recommended paper, see pp. 209–212.

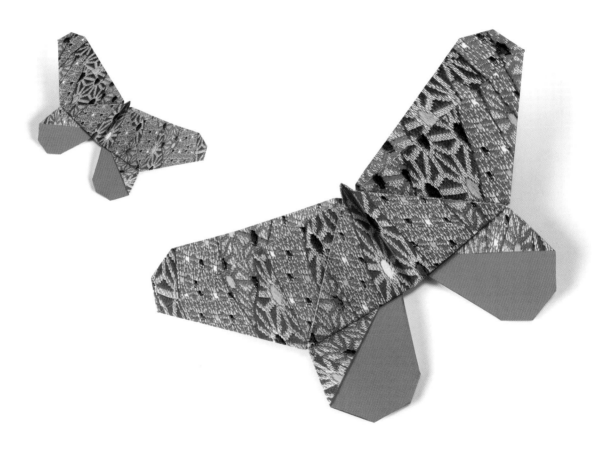

butterfly > **70**

1. **Fold** a strip approximately 3cm (1¼in) wide.

2. **Fold down** by joining up the dots.

3. **Mark** the crease on the right and make a reverse fold (see p. 9), as on the left side, then fold the left part downwards and flatten. On the top edge, fold the strips down to the back.

4. **Fold down** the left side, then tilt the top edge to the front beneath the thickness.

5. **Fold over** the top and bottom tips, then lift the centre part up behind by joining up the dots.

6. **Crease** the centre to give the butterfly volume.

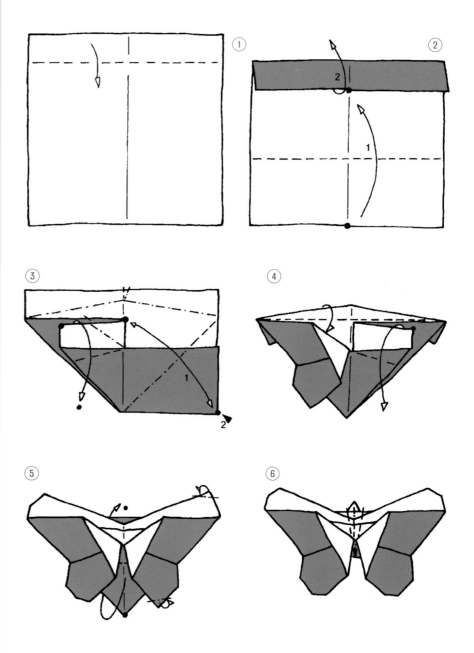

Owl

At nightfall, the owl slips on his feathered coat and goes out for a night on the town! What a hoot!

For recommended paper, see pp. 213–220.

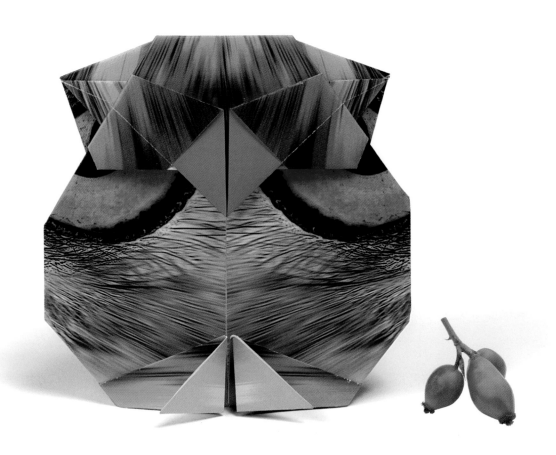

1. **Fold down** the sides onto the centre marks.

2. **Fold** the sides into the centre then unfold the bottom.

3. **Fold** the four corners.

4. **Fold** the top in half and unfold the bottom part.

5. **Open** the top triangle and flatten. On the bottom part, lift up the left side by joining up the dots.

6. **Repeat** on the other side.

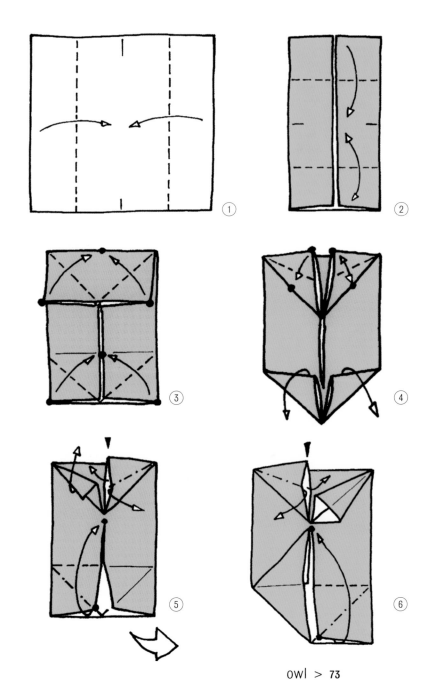

Owl (cont.)

7 **Lift up** the top part and fold the bottom triangle behind.

8 **Fold** as indicated on the left (1), then fold down (2) on both sides. Fold the right triangle as indicated.

9 **Make** the ears appear by making a pleat fold (see p. 8) in the top corners. To finish off the feet, fold the right tip then pleat fold in the same way on the other side.

10 **Round off** the body by folding back the sides.

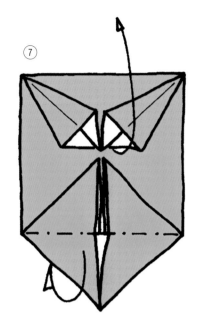

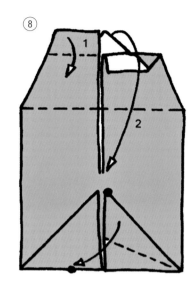

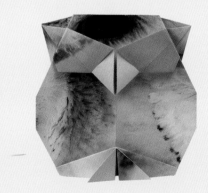

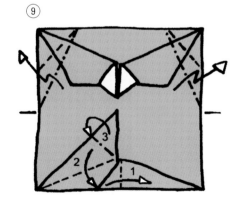

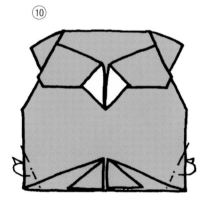

Bird card

This migrating bird flies off into the sky to send a special little message to the four corners of the world.

For recommended paper, see pp. 221–224.

Bird card (cont.)

1 **Mark** the quarter crease then mark the right corner.

2 **Fold** the corner then lift up the strip.

3 **Fold** the top corner, then fold over as indicated.

4 **Fold down** the right side.

5 **Fold** the left part back.

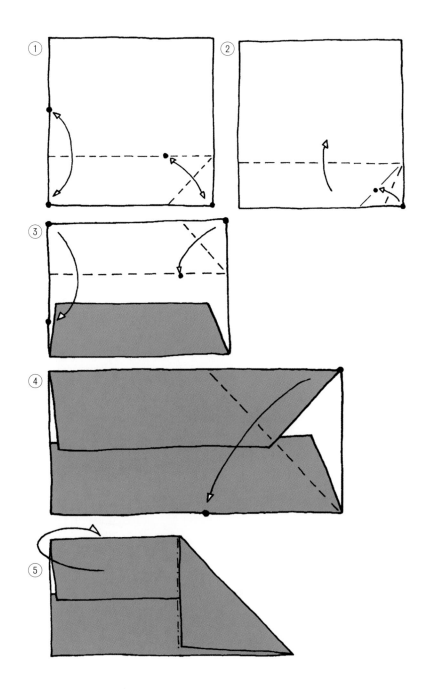

6. **Lift up** the tip vertically.
7. **Open** then flatten.
8. **Mark** the sides.
9. **Lift up** the tip making a half bird base (see p. 11).
10. **Fold** in half.
11. **Form** the wing by lifting up the left part along the top edge. To finish the head, make a reverse fold (see p. 9) on the tip.

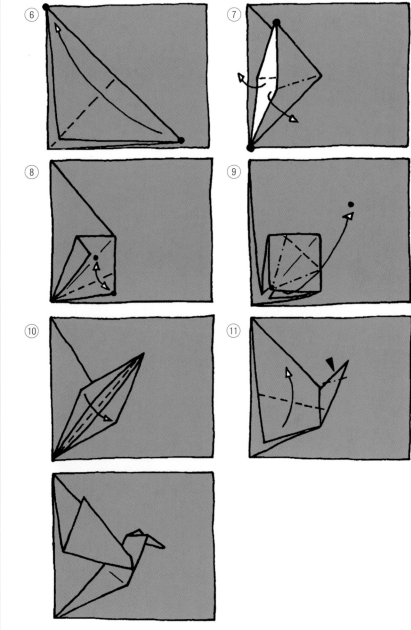

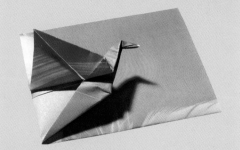

Turtledove

With its wild plumage, the turtledove lives away from the town, in contrast to its cousin, the pigeon.

For recommended paper, see pp. 225–228.

1. **Fold** the bird base (see p. 11), then fold in half.

2. **Form** the legs by opening and flattening the triangles on both faces.

Detail for the legs

2a. **Fold** towards the top, inverting the sides.

2b. **Fold** in half.

2c. **Lift up** the front in a reverse fold (see p. 9).

3. **Fold in** the rear tip. To make the legs, make a reverse fold and fold over the angular parts. To form the head, make a pleat fold.

4. **Fold down** the wings and reduce the neck.

5. **Finish** the rear by folding in the order indicated (1, 2, 3). To make the beak, make a pleat fold and fold the tip over.

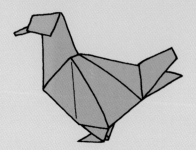

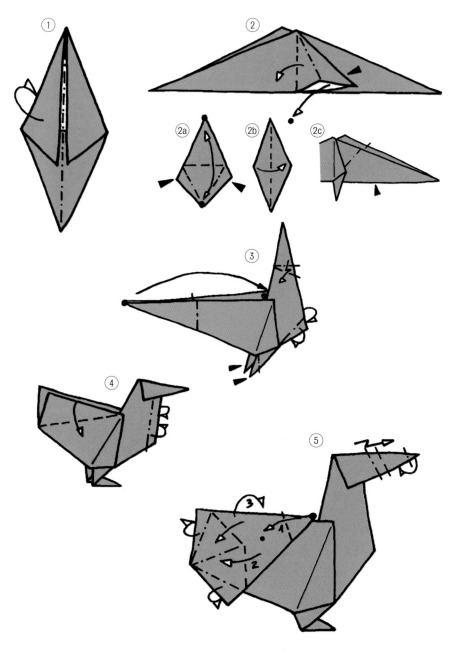

Sparrow

In the spring, you'll see sparrows sitting on the electric power cables; they're enjoying swinging to and fro and telling each other about their adventures.

For recommended paper, see pp. 229–232.

1. **Fold** a preliminary base (see p. 10) and a half bird base (see p. 11) then turn over.

2. **Cut** the top sheet along the bold line.

3. **Fold** in half.

4. **Make** a reverse fold (see p. 9) at the front, then lift up the tip as indicated.

5. **Form** the head by making a reverse fold. At the rear, fold both tips to the inside then lift up the wings

6. **Move apart** the sides for the head. Fold the legs back in half.

7. **Form** the beak by making a pleat fold (see p. 8). Fold over the angular parts, then form the legs (see p. 11).

To find the sparrow's balancing point, adjust the position of it's legs or slip a piece of wire inside them.

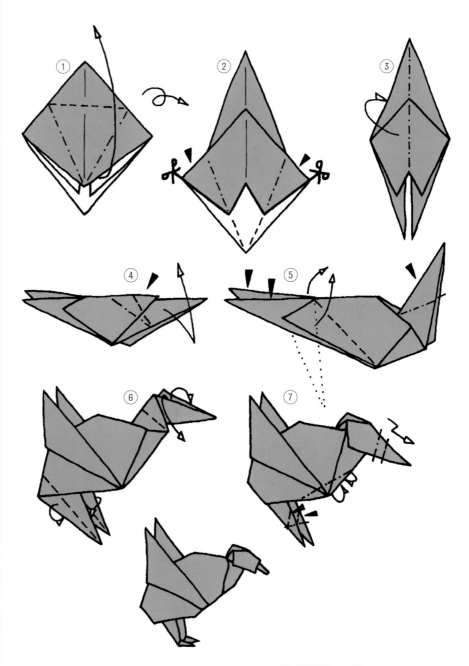

Tropical bird

In the courting season, this vibrantly-coloured bird sings and shows off its magnificent plumage.

For recommended paper, see pp. 233–236.

1. **Mark** the horizontal crease, then fold in half to the right.

2. **Fold** along the creases indicated.

3. **Fold** the bottom part in half and unfold the top part.

4. **Unfold** everything.

5. **Fold** in half downwards.

6. **Fold** the first thickness, lifting the two sides.

7. **Flatten**, then turn over.

8. **Push in** the sides, inverting the folds.

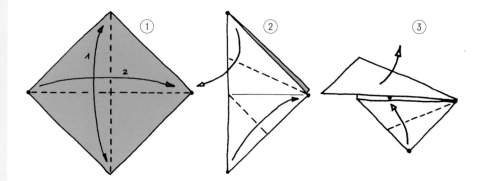

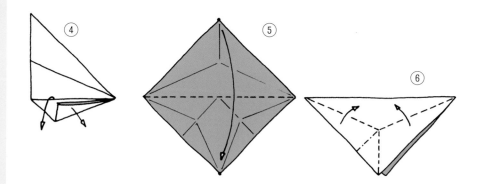

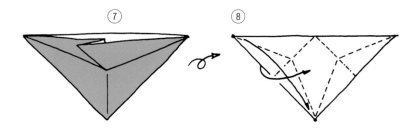

tropical bird > **83**

Tropical bird (cont.)

9 **Join** the tips at the bottom.

10 **Lift up** the tips.

11 **Make** the legs by marking the creases, folding along the dotted lines.

12 **Open** each tip, then fold them down flat on each side.

Detail for the legs

12a **Slim down** the legs by folding over the sides, leaving a space in the centre.

12b **Fold** in half upwards.

13 **Fold** in half to give volume.

14 **After pre-creasing**, make an outside reverse fold (see p. 9) by opening the tip.

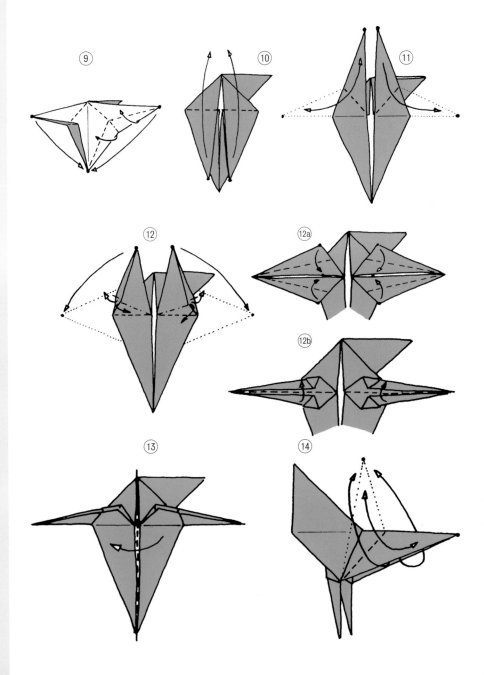

15 **Make** the tail by marking the crease of the left tip. To form the head, make an outside reverse fold. For the legs, mark the crease, then make an inside reverse fold.

16 **Form** the tail by opening the tip, then flattenning on each side. For the head, unfold the inside part on each face. For the legs, make another reverse fold.

Detail for the legs

16a **Mark** the creases, then open the tip.

16b **Put** the top sides into a mountain fold (see p. 8), then lift up the tip.

16c **Tilt** the tip forward folding the leg in half.

Detail for the head

17a **Fold** the tip.

17b **Fold** the tip over, then unfold it.

17c **Make** a pleat fold (see p. 8) by opening the tip.

17d **Check** your model is as shown from above.

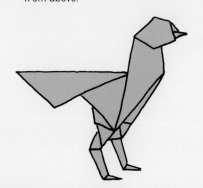

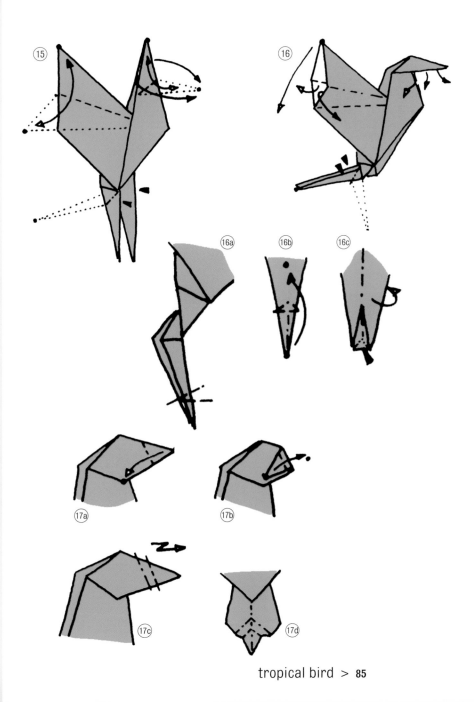

tropical bird > **85**

Hamster

The hamster is an affectionate little pet who munches on everything in his path.

For recommended paper, see pp. 237–240.

1. **Mark** the centre crease.

2. **Fold** in half upwards.

3. **Fold over** the top triangle to create the ears.

4. **Fold over** another little triangle to create the muzzle.

5. **Check** your model is as shown, then turn over.

6. **Fold** the tips towards the outside to form the legs.

7. **Slim down** the legs by folding them in half.

8. **Fold** everything in half.

9. **Lift up** the ears. To form the tail, fold over the corner.

10. **Separate** the ears using scissors. For the tail, make a backwards pleat fold (see p. 8).

Detail for the tail

10a **Unfold**.

10b **Make** an inside reverse fold (see p. 9)

10c **...by opening** the fold slightly,

10d **...then lifting up** the little triangle towards the outside to make it stick out.

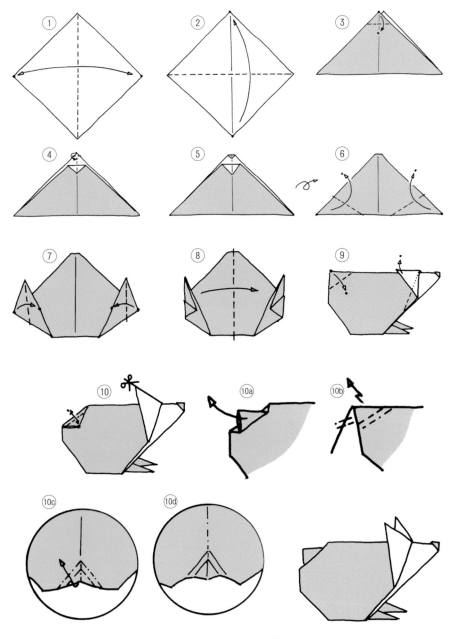

hamster > **87**

Tree frog

The tree frog lives on the edge of the water where it practises underwater diving with it's beautiful pair of webbed feet.

For recommended paper, see pp. 241–244.

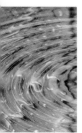

1. **Make** a water bomb base (see p. 10), then fold over the sides as on the left and fold the left leg in half.

2. **Fold** the right leg in the same way, then unfold the sides.

3. **Lift up** the sides, keeping to the creases indicated. Fold over the right side.

4. **Fold** the left side. To make the forelegs, fold the tips on the sides as on the right, then fold over the tips. Turn everything over.

5. **Fold over** the rear on each side, then unfold.

6. **Fold over** pushing in the sides.

7. **Lift** up the legs from behind and fold over the ends to finish. At the front, fold over the tip, then curve the top part for the eyes.

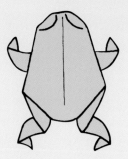

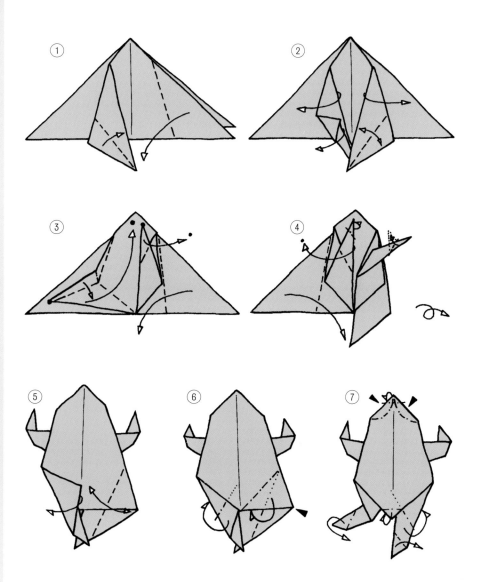

tree frog > **89**

Snail

By day, the snail slowly and steadily exlores the world around him. In the evening, he nibbles on a lettuce leaf and retreats into his shell.

For recommended paper, see pp. 245–248.

1 **Fold over** the sides onto the centre crease.

2 **Fold** in half behind.

3 **Mark** the crease by joining up the dots.

4 **Make** an outside reverse fold (see p. 9).

5 **Fold** in half by joining up the dots.

6 **Fold** in half as indicated.

7 **Fold over** in half again, then cut along the bold line.

8 **Fold** in half one last time, slipping the end between the thicknesses. To form the horns, fold the tips in half then lift them upwards.

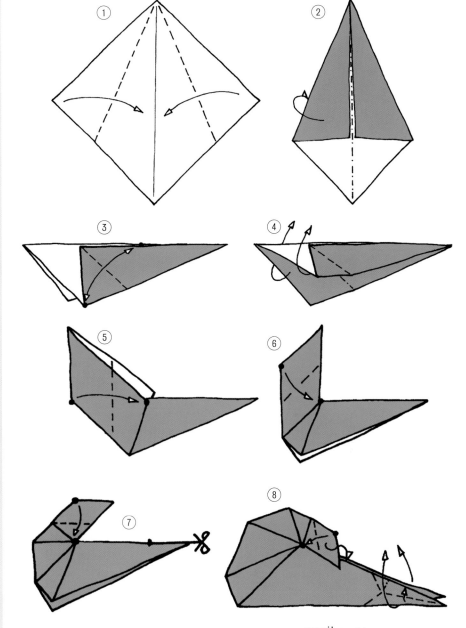

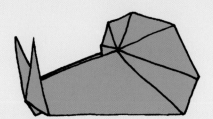

snail > **91**

Marvellous mascots...

Cat and leopard

The leopard is dressed in a fine robe and walks around nonchalantly, whilst the cat, dressed in a beautiful spotted robe, watches on.

For recommended papers, see pp. 249–264.
Use two squares of paper for each mascot.

THE LEOPARD'S HEAD

1 **Take** a square measuring 11.5cm (4½in), then fold down by joining up the dots.

2 **Fold** the sides to the horizontal dotted line (see fish base, p. 13).

3 **Open** the centre triangle then flatten to form the nose. To form the ears, lift up the sides behind.

4 **Check** your model is as shown.

5 **Fold** the edges of the nose behind, then fold down the top part. To make the end of the nose, fold over the triangle a little.

6 **Give** volume to the ears, as on the left, then fold down behind the top tip. Reduce the sides by folding behind, as on the left.
Give volume to the muzzle by making a pleat fold (see p. 8) on each side, then cut and fold the little triangles behind for the chops.

Here is the leopard's head:

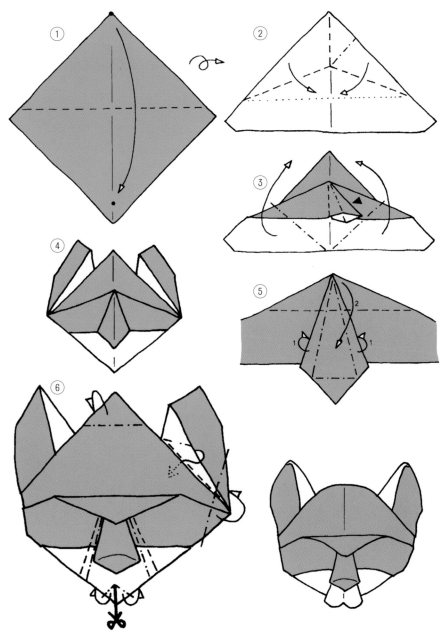

Cat and leopard
(cont.)

THE CAT'S HEAD

1 **Take** a square measuring 13cm (5in).
   Fold stages 1 to 4 of the Bulldog (see
   p. 99). Then fold the sides in two moves,
   as on the left.

2 **Mark** the crease of the top tip.

3 **Open** this tip, turning back the triangles
   onto the sides.

3a **Check** your model is as shown, then
   turn over.

4 **Form** the muzzle by folding over the
   centre tip. Fold the bottom tips towards
   the back.

5 **Fold** the edges underneath as indicated
   to finish off the muzzle.

Here is the cat's head:

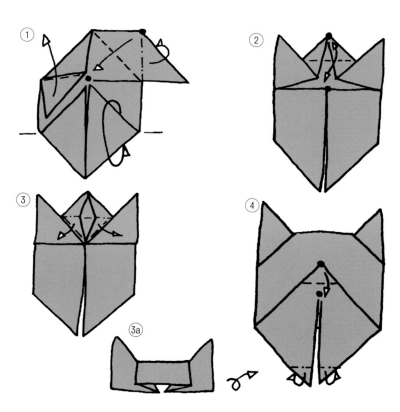

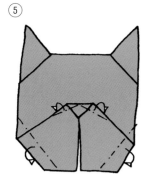

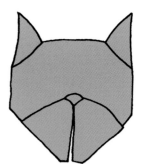

THE CAT AND THE LEOPARD'S BODIES

1 **Fold** the side onto the centre.

2 **Fold over** by joining up the dots.

3 **Fold** in half as indicated then unfold to the right.

4 **Fold over** the left part then fold the right side into the centre.

5 **Fold over** into three as far as the centre.

6 **Lift up** the tip behind then turn over.

7 **Fold over** the sides as far as the centre.

8 **Form** the tail by folding the tip down as indicated then turn over.

Place a head on the tip:

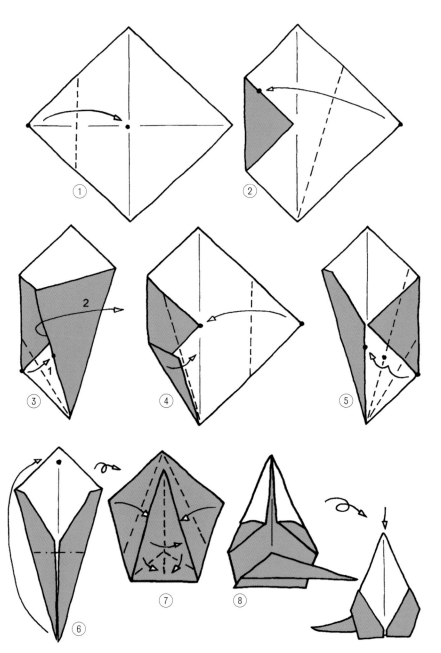

Bulldog

The bulldog is a heavy, muscular dog with a distictinctive pushed-in nose, popularly used to represent England and all that is British.

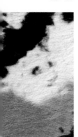

For recommended papers, see pp. 265–272.
Use two squares of paper.

HEAD

1 **Fold** the sides as indicated.

2 **Fold** the top corners behind and the bottom corners in front.

3 **Bring** the top part to the front and mark the crease on the bottom part then unfold the corners.

4 **Pull** the top triangles towards the outside and lift up the bottom part by joining up the dots.

5 **Fold over** the sides as on the left, then tilt the bottom part along the axis indicated.

6 **Form** the ears by lifting up the tips as on the left then folding over the little triangles on each side. Fold the bottom part in half and turn over.

7 **Form** the end of the nose by folding down the tip by opening it.

Here is the bulldog's head:

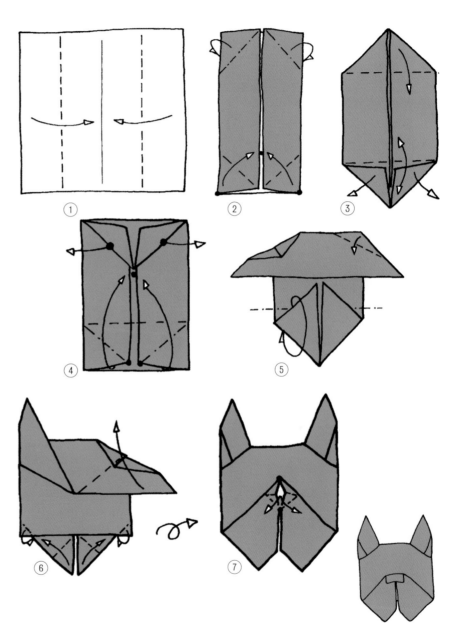

Bulldog (cont.)

BODY

1 **Fold** in half.

2 **Fold over** a strip on each side.

3 **Open** in half.

4 **Fold over** the four corners.

5 **Fold over** the sides.

6 **Pull** the sides towards the outside.

Here is the bulldog's body:

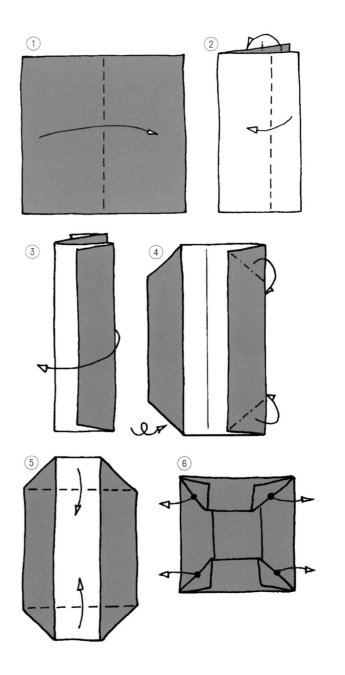

7 **Check** your model is as shown then
turn over.

8 **Fold** the sides as on the left then
turn over.

9 **Fold over** the triangle then fold in
half behind.

10 **Make** a reverse fold (see p. 9) at the
rear then fold over an edge to finish the
stomach. At the front, make a flattened
fold to hold the bulldog's head.

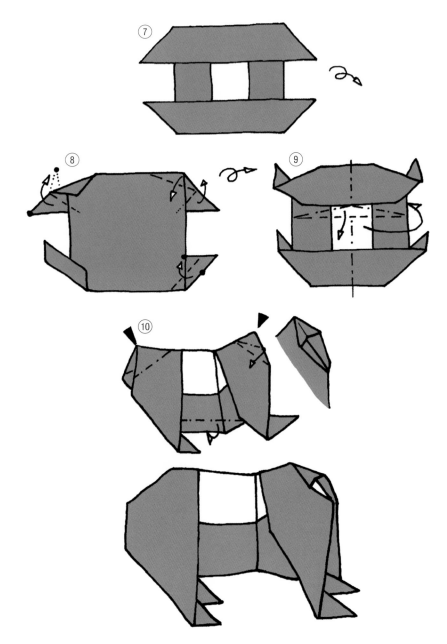

Bear cub

This smiling bear cub is dressed up warmly to protect its little, round stomach from the wintry weather.

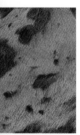

For recommended papers: see pp. 273–280.
Use two squares of paper.

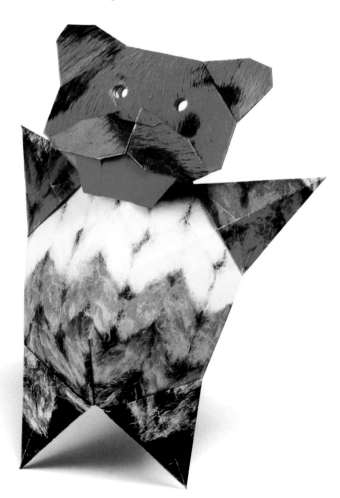

HEAD

1. **Take** a square measuring 14.5cm (5¾in). Fold the sides, then turn over.

2. **Mark** the creases, then turn over.

3. **Fold** the top triangles, as on the left, folding down the sides behind.

4. **Check** your model is as shown, then turn over.

5. **Fold over** the inside tips of the ears, then fold the centre part as on the left.

6. **Lift up** the corners.

7. **Lift** the bottom part up to the rear. To finish the ears, fold the tip inside then fold over the edge as on the left.

8. **Lift up** the sides as on the left, then turn over.

9. **Form** the nose by rolling up the tip.

Detail

9a. **Fold** the top edges down behind, then fold under the bottom corners.

Here is the bear cub's head:

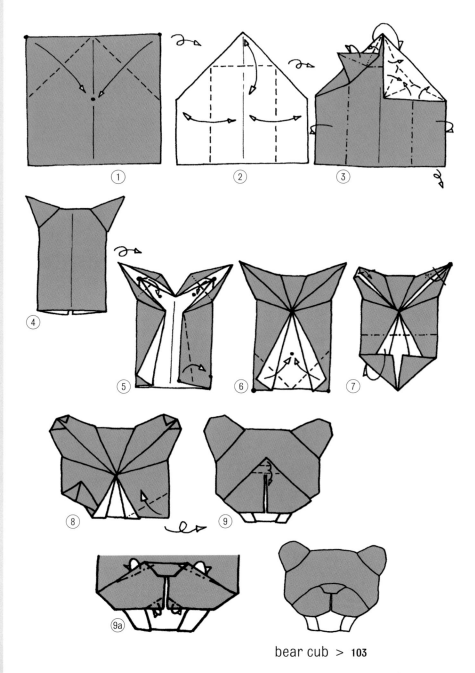

bear cub > **103**

Bear cub (cont.)

BODY

1 **Fold** the sides.

2 **Fold over** the corners behind, then fold everything over to the front.

3 **Unfold**, pulling towards the outside.

4 **Fold** the four tips like the one on the left, then fold over towards the centre making a reverse fold (see p. 9).

5 **Unfold** completely then turn over.

6 **Fold over** the four corners into the centre.

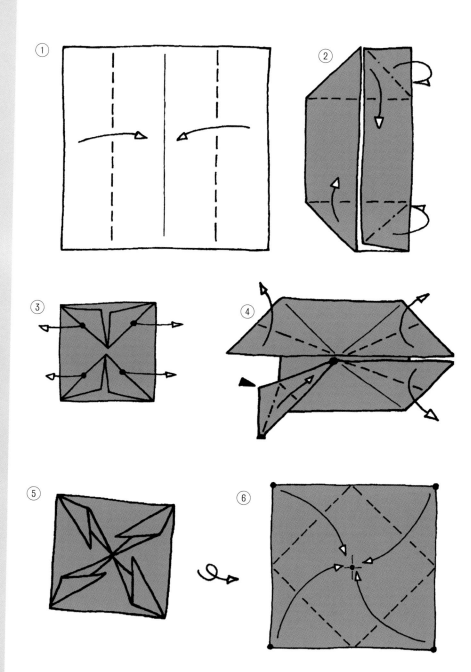

7 **Fold over** each side as indicated, folding back each corner behind.

8 **Lift up** the top tip from the back as indicated, then completely draw down the one at the bottom.

9 **Give** volume to his stomach by folding the centre crease in half. Fold down the tip underneath.

10 **Place** the head of the bear cub in the place indicated.

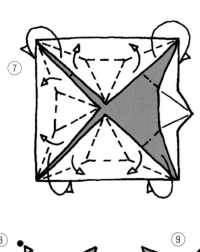

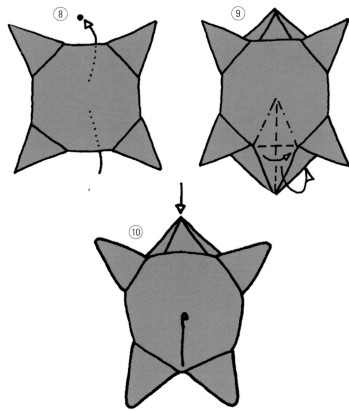

Three little rabbits

These quirky rabbits with quivering ears have an assortment of colourful coats to wear for each season. Experiment by matching the little heads to different bodies for fun results.

For recommended papers, see pp. 281–320. Use two squares of paper for each mascot.

OPEN-MOUTHED RABBIT

1 **Take** a square measuring 14.5cm (5¾in) and fold the sides.

2 **Fold** the corners behind, then fold everything over to the front.

3 **Unfold**, pulling towards the outside.

4 **Lift up** the centre at the same time as the two tips.

5 **Fold** one side.

6 **Fold down** near the top and flatten.

7 **Repeat** for the right side, then make a pleat fold (see p. 8).

8 **Fold** the sides as on the right.

Detail for the mouth

8a **Lift up** the sides underneath the triangles.

8b **Fold over** the two edges.

8c **Check** your model is as shown then turn over.

Here is the finished head:

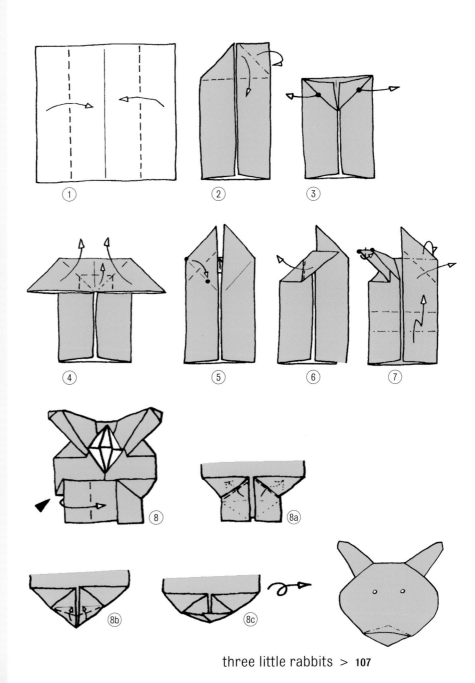

three little rabbits > **107**

Three little rabbits (cont.)

RABBIT WITH BIG EARS

1 **Take** a square measuring 11.5cm (4½in) then fold the sides.

2 **Fold** the corners behind, then fold everything over to the front.

3 **Unfold** by pulling towards the outside.

4 **Fold** the tips as on the left then lift them up as indicated. Lift up the bottom part.

5 **Fold down** leaving a fairly wide strip (a quarter of the width).

6 **Form the neck** by folding over the sides as on the right then turning over.

7 **Cut** along the bold line to finish.

Here is the finished head:

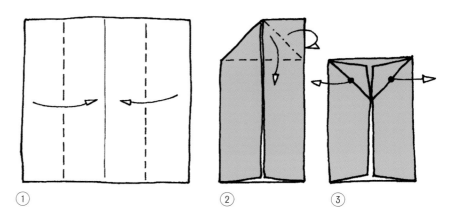

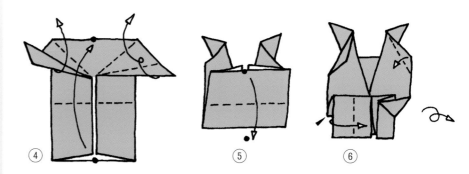

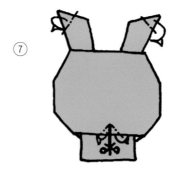

three little rabbits > 108

RABBIT WITH BIG EYES

1 **Take** a square measuring 15cm (6in) and fold the sides.

2 **Fold** the corners behind then fold everything over to the front.

3 **Unfold** by pulling towards the outside as indicated.

4 **Lift up** the tips as on the left then open the bottom triangles and fold the little squares in half.

Detail

4a **Lift up** the centre part then lift up the tips.

5 **Fold** the tips on the top part and fold down the sides. Lift up behind by joining up the dots then turn over.

6 **Form the eyes** by folding underneath as indicated then make a valley fold (see p. 8) at the base.

6a **Fold** over the triangles to finish the eyes.

Here is the head with big eyes:

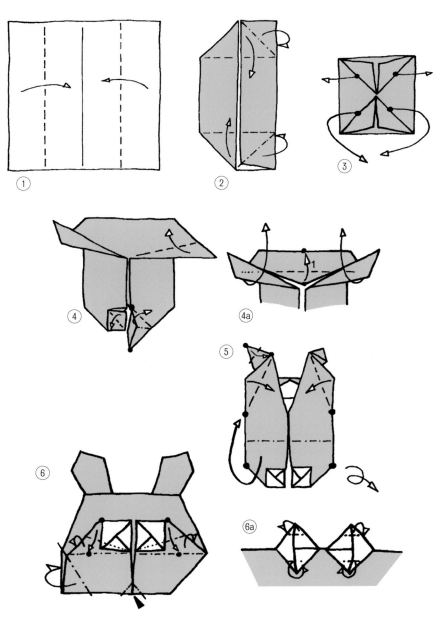

three little rabbits > 109

Three little rabbits (cont.)

BODY 1

1 **Fold over**, joining up the centres then turn over.

2 **Fold over** the bottom corners, then fold over the sides onto the centre crease, pressing down on the left corner.

3 **Open** the right side towards the outside.

4 **Form the arms** by folding over the sides and folding the base onto the centre.

5 **Pull** the two parts downwards.

6 **Slip** in a strip of paper for placing on a head of your choice, then turn over.

7 **Insert** the rabbit's head on a strip by cutting the top of the body.

Assembly strip

a **Fold** the sides of a strip measuring 8 x 16cm (3½ x 6¼in).

b **Fold** the corners.

c **Fold over** once.

d **This strip** links a body with a head.

Here is the finished body:

three little rabbits > 110

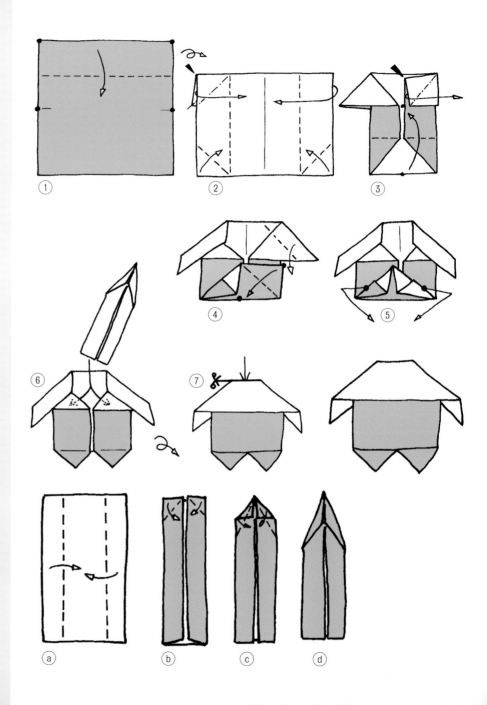

BODY 2

1 **Fold down** the sides onto the centre crease.

2 **Check** as shown, then turn over.

3 **Fold over** the sides.

4 **Fold** in half.

5 **Fold over** the sides.

6 **Pull** towards the outside.

7 **Fold** the sides as on the left, then fold over downwards.

8 **Tilt** the sides to the front as on the left then, to form the feet, fold over the sides.

9 **Fold down** the top and make a pleat fold (see p. 8) at the feet.

10 **Roll up** towards the top.

11 **Insert** a head, then fold down the arms towards the centre. If necessary, slip an assembly strip behind (see p. 110).

Here is the finished body:

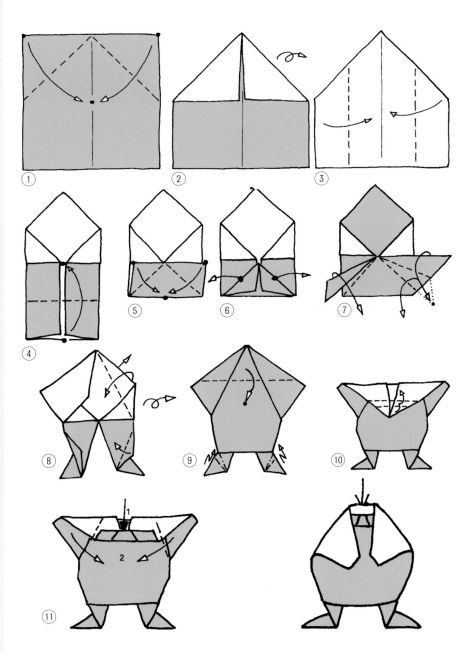

Three little rabbits (cont.)

BODY 3

1 **Make** a water bomb base (see p. 10) then lift up two sides.

2 **Draw down** the tips by joining up the dots.

3 **Turn** to the right.

4 **Fold over** the left side along the centre crease, then fold the left part by joining up the dots.

5 **Fold down** the tip to the right then fold the bottom in half.

6 **Turn** towards the left.

7 **Fold over** the right side then join up the dots by folding.

8 **Fold down** the other point towards the left then fold the bottom in half.

9 **Turn** to the right then turn over.

10 **Form** the feet by folding the tip.

Detail for the feet

10a **Fold over** the tip on the left.

10b **Unfold**.

10c **Fold** the legs following the instructions on p. 11.

Place a head of your choice, on the tip of the body:

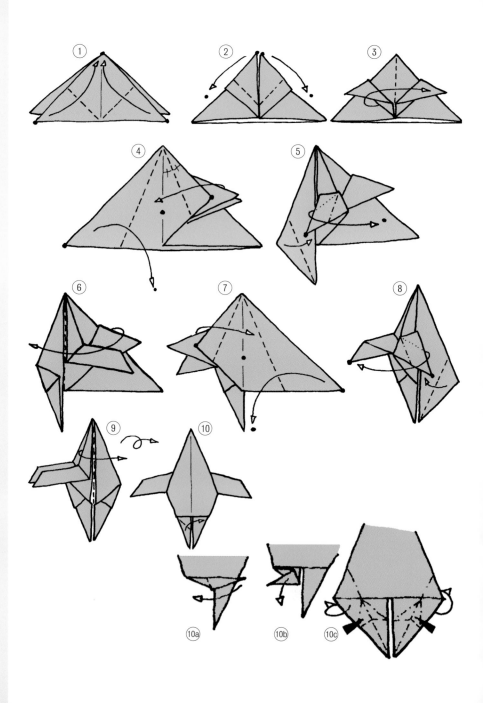

Young cow and bull-calf

Young cows and bull-calves love to chew on blades of grass in the fields as they watch the trains go by.

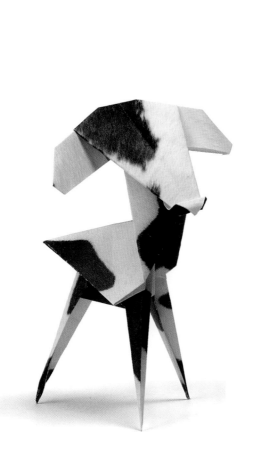

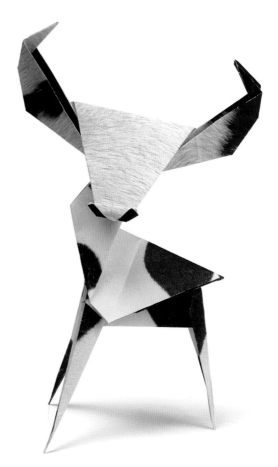

See pp. 321–332.
Use two squares of paper for each mascot.

Young cow and bull-calf

(cont.)

THE YOUNG COW HEAD

1 **Take** a square measuring 10.5cm (5¾in) that can be matched up with the body, then fold in half.

2 **Lift up** the tips.

3 **Fold** by joining up the dots, then turn over.

4 **Lift up** the sides as on the left then fold the bottom part towards the outside.

5 **Fold** the sides downwards, as on the left, then fold the top left part.

6 **Fold down** the other side, then fold the two tips of the ears and turn over.

7 **Fold** the top part to finish.

Here is the finished young cow's head:

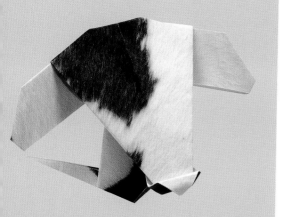

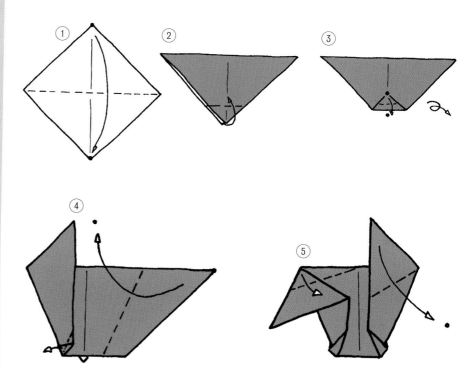

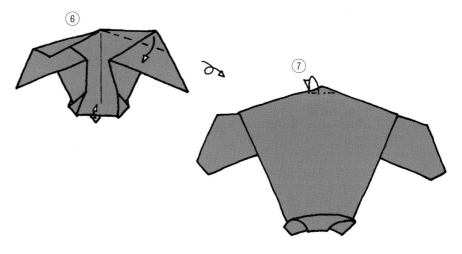

THE BULL-CALF'S HEAD

1 **Take** a square measuring 10.5cm (5¾in) that can be matched up with the body, then fold in half.

2 **Fold** the tip as indicated and turn over.

3 **Lift up** the sides as on the left, then make a reverse fold (see p. 9) in the two tips. Fold the bottom part towards the outside.

4 **Form** the horns by bringing the tips down to a horizontal position.

5 **Check** your model is as shown then turn over.

6 **Lift up** the horns as on the left then make a reverse fold in the ends. To finish the nostrils, fold over the bottom tip, curving everything.

Here is the finished bull-calf's head:

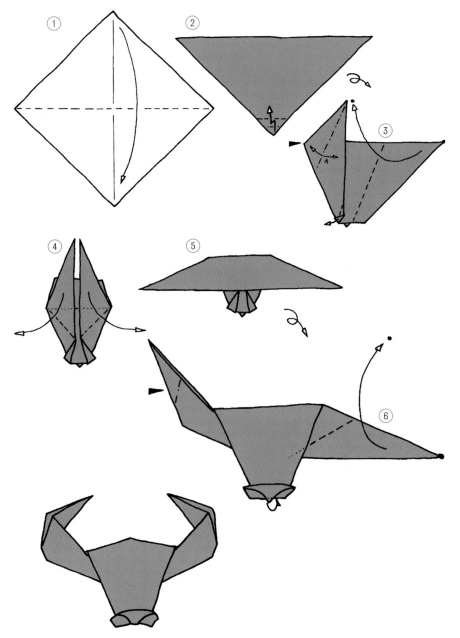

young cow and bull-calf > 115

Young cow and bull-calf

(cont.)

THE YOUNG COW AND BULL-CALF'S BODY:

1 **Fold** a bird base (see p. 11), then open the sides and flatten them as on the right.

2 **Fold over** the tips then lift up the rear tip.

3 **Fold** in half.

4 **Form** the neck by making an outside reverse fold (see p. 9) of the right tip to be folded. At the rear, make a reverse fold to make the hind leg.

4a **Reduce** the tip by folding it over.

4b **Fold over** to the front on each side.

Here is the body of the young cow or the bull-calf:

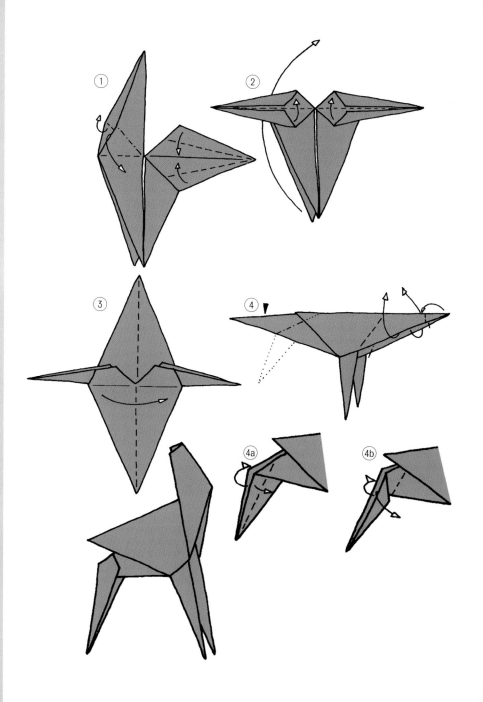

Mix and match the heads and bodies!

mix and match the heads and bodies > 118

Papers

On the following pages, you'll find the papers that have been used to make the models presented in this book. There are also some extra papers, which means you can let your imagination run riot and discover the wealth of expression available to you through origami!

Recommended paper for the Arabian horse: see instructions and instructions on pp. 16–17

Recommended paper for the Arabian horse: see diagrams and instructions on pp. 16–17

Recommended paper for the Desert lizard: see diagrams and instructions on pp. 18–19

Recommended paper for the Desert lizard: see diagrams and instructions on pp. 18–19

Recommended paper for the Desert fox cub: see diagrams and instructions on pp. 20–22

Recommended paper for the **Elephant calf:** see diagrams and instructions on pp. 26–27

Recommended paper for the Elephant calf: see diagrams and instructions on pp. 26–27

Recommended paper for the Monkey: see diagrams and instructions on pp. 28–29

Recommended paper for the **Monkey:** see diagrams and instructions on pp. 28–29

47

Recommended paper for the **Bear**: see diagrams and instructions on pp. 30–31

Recommended paper for the Bear: see diagrams and instructions on pp. 30–31

Recommended paper for the Whale: see diagrams and instructions on pp. 32–33

53

Recommended paper for the Little Fish: see diagrams and instructions on pp. 54–55

Recommended paper for the Little fish: see diagrams and instructions on pp. 54–55

Recommended paper for the Inflatable fish: see diagrams and instructions on pp. 36–37

Recommended paper for the Goose: see diagrams and instructions on pp. 40–42

Recommended paper for the **Goose**: see diagrams and instructions on pp. 40–42

Recommended paper for the **Pig**: see diagrams and instructions on pp. 43–45

Recommended paper for the Ram: see diagrams and instructions on pp. 40–45

Recommended paper for the Ram: see diagrams and instructions on pp. 46–49

Recommended paper for the Duck: see diagrams and instructions on pp. 50–51

Recommended paper for the Goat: see diagrams and instructions on pp. 32–35

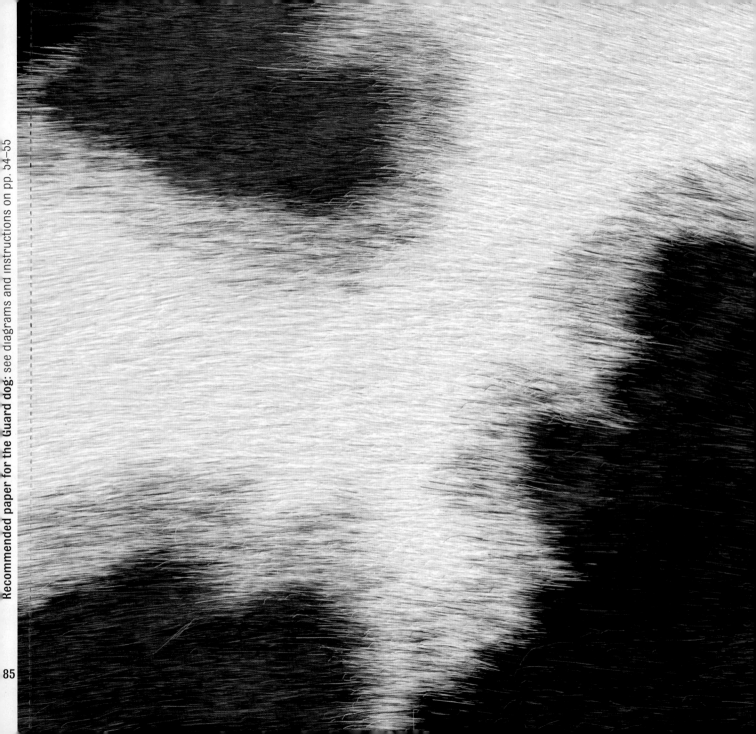

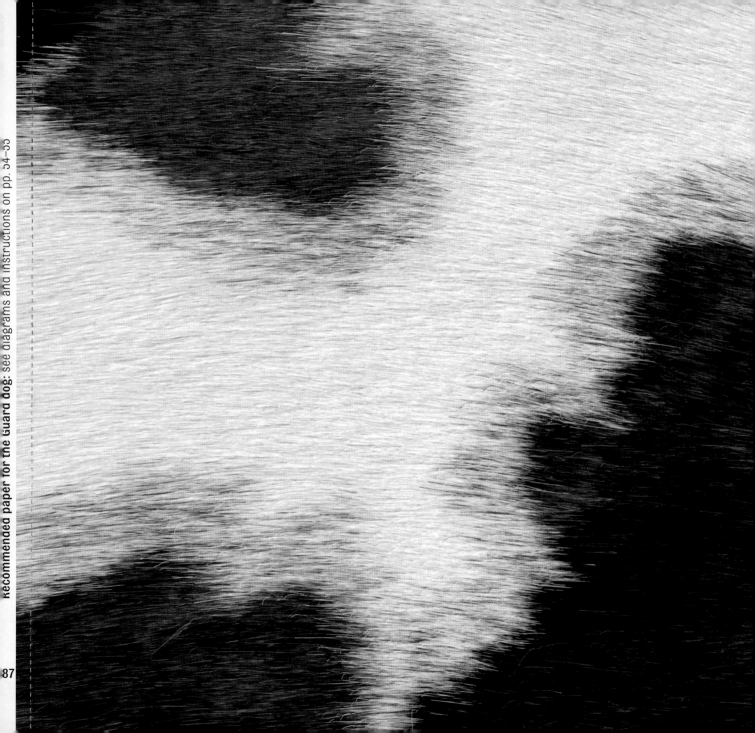

Recommended paper for the Hare: see diagrams and instructions on pp. 58–59

Recommended paper for the Hare: see diagrams and instructions on pp. 58–59

Recommended paper for the Peacock: see diagrams and instructions on pp. 60–61

Recommended paper for the Peacock: see diagrams and instructions on pp. 60–61

Recommended paper for the Swan: see diagrams and instructions on pp. 64–66

01

Recommended paper for the Swan: see diagrams and instructions on pp. 64–66

Recommended paper for the **Dragonfly**: see diagrams and instructions on pp. 67–69

Recommended paper for the **Dragonfly:** see diagrams and instructions on pp. 67–69

Recommended paper for the Butterfly: see diagrams and instructions on pp. 70–71

Recommended paper for the Butterfly: see diagrams and instructions on pp. 70–71

Recommended paper for the Owl: see diagrams and instructions on pp. 72–74

Recommended paper for the Owl: see diagrams and instructions on pp. 72–74

17

Recommended paper for the owl: see diagrams and instructions on pp. 12–14

19

Recommended paper for the Bird card: see diagrams and instructions on pp. 75–77

Recommended paper for the **Bird card**: see diagrams and instructions on pp. 75–77

Recommended paper for the Turtledove: see diagrams and instructions on pp. 78–79

Recommended paper for the Turtledove: see diagrams and instructions on pp. 78–79

Recommended paper for the Sparrow: see diagrams and instructions on pp. 80–81

Recommended paper for the Sparrow: see diagrams and instructions on pp. 80–81

Recommended paper for the Tropical bird. See diagrams and instructions on pp. 62–66

35

Recommended paper for the Hamster: see diagrams and instructions on pp. 86–87

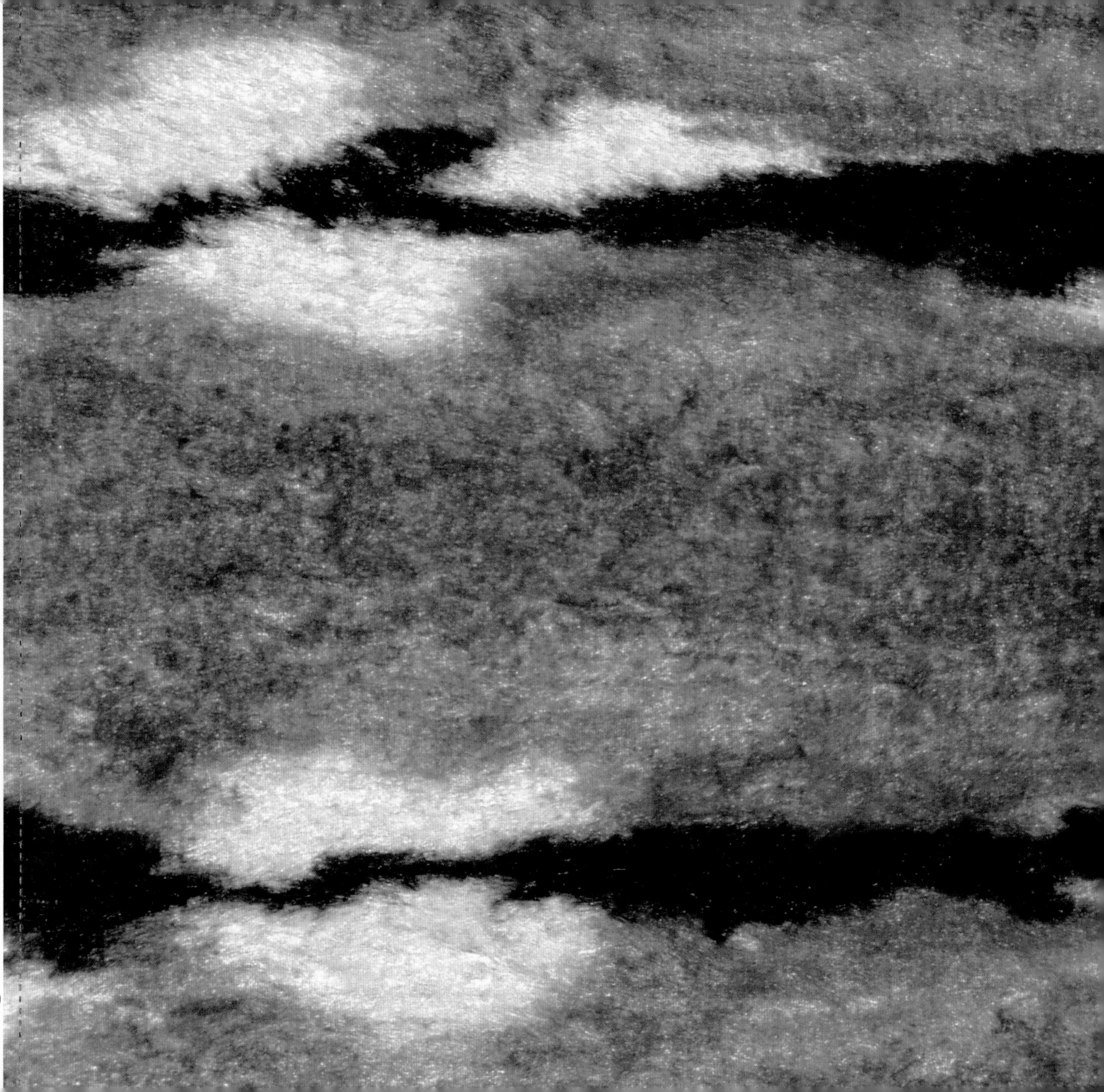

Recommended paper for the Hamster: see diagrams and instructions on pp. 86–87

Recommended paper for the Tree frog: see diagrams and instructions on pp. 88–89

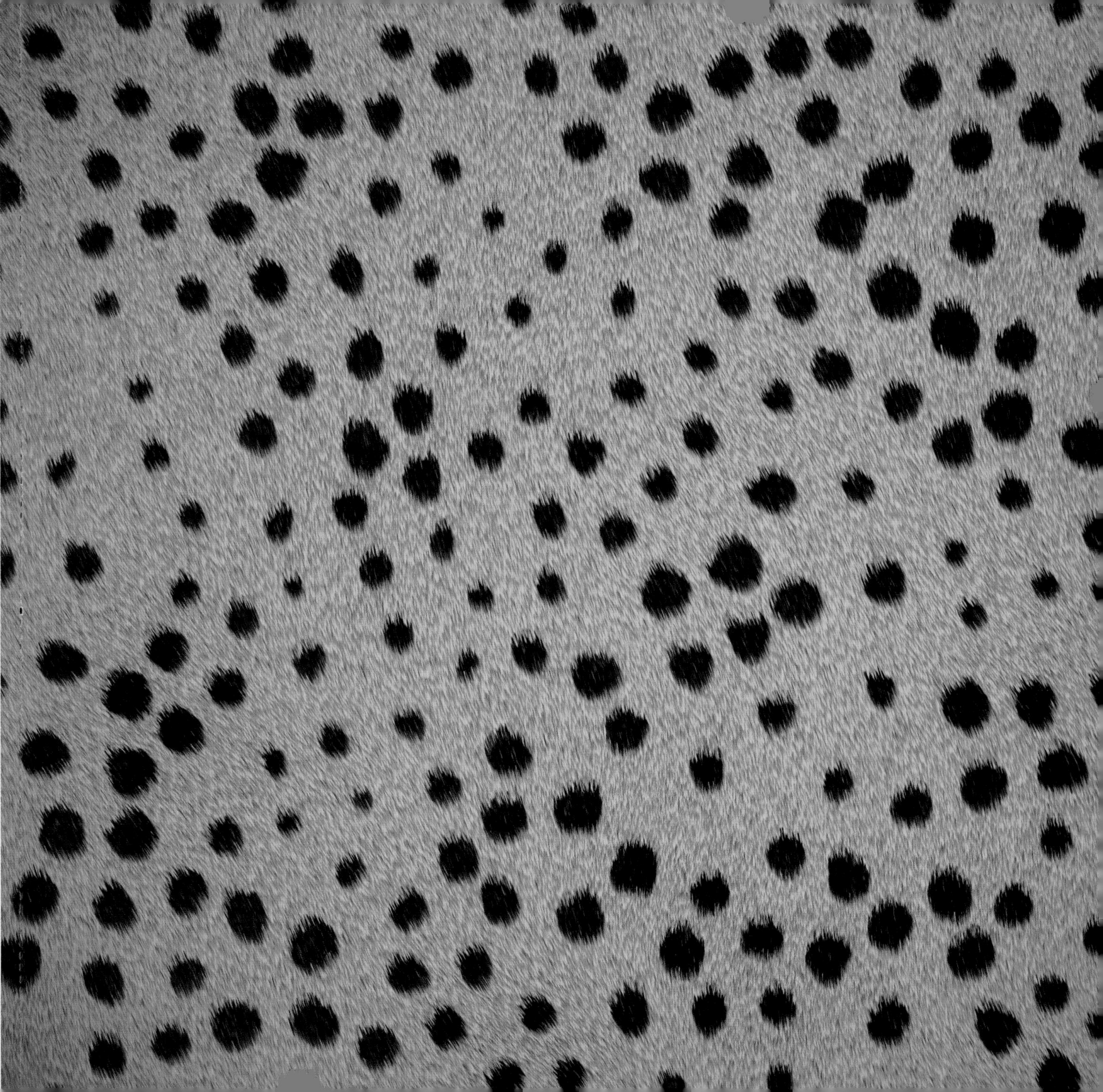

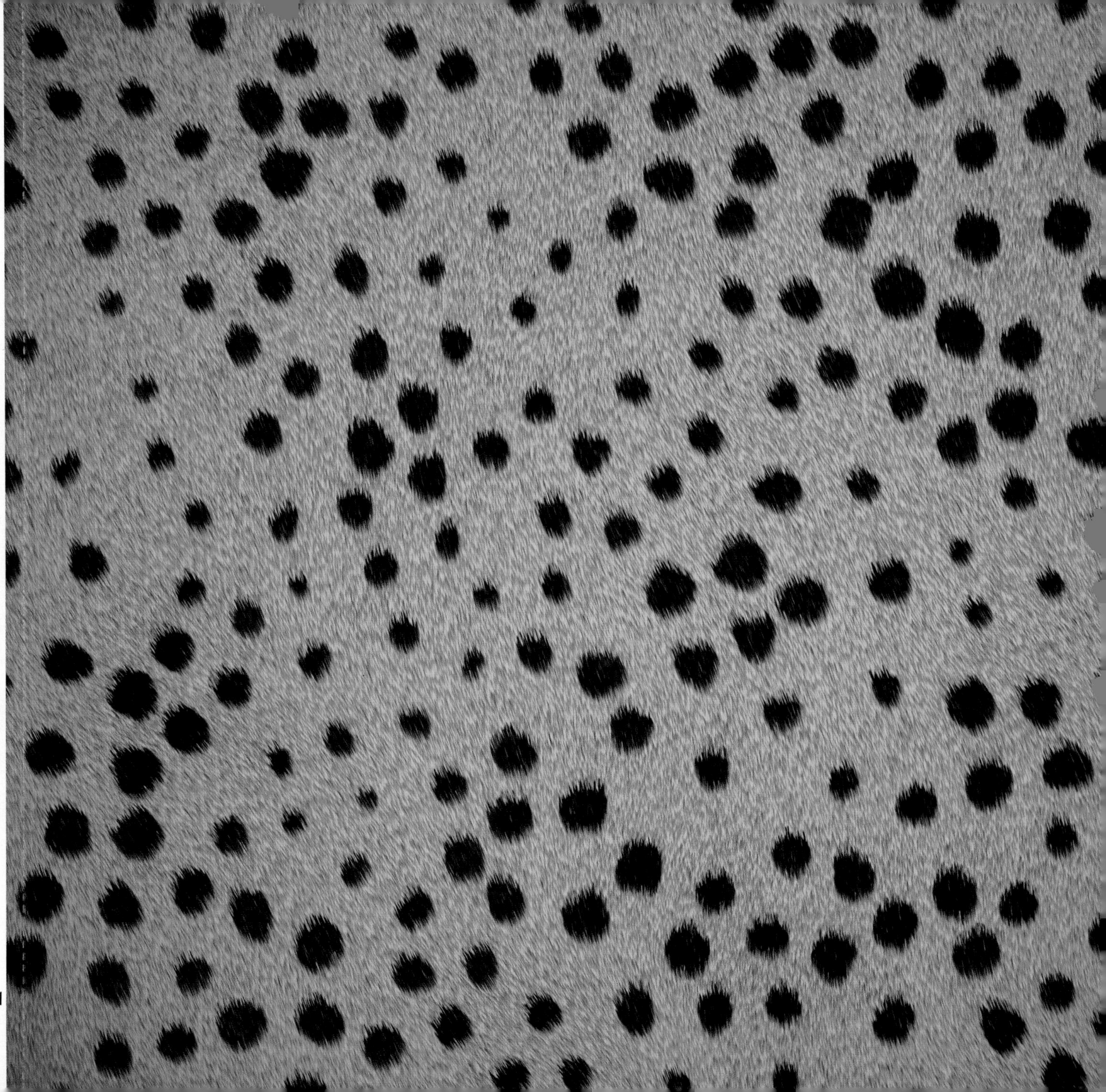

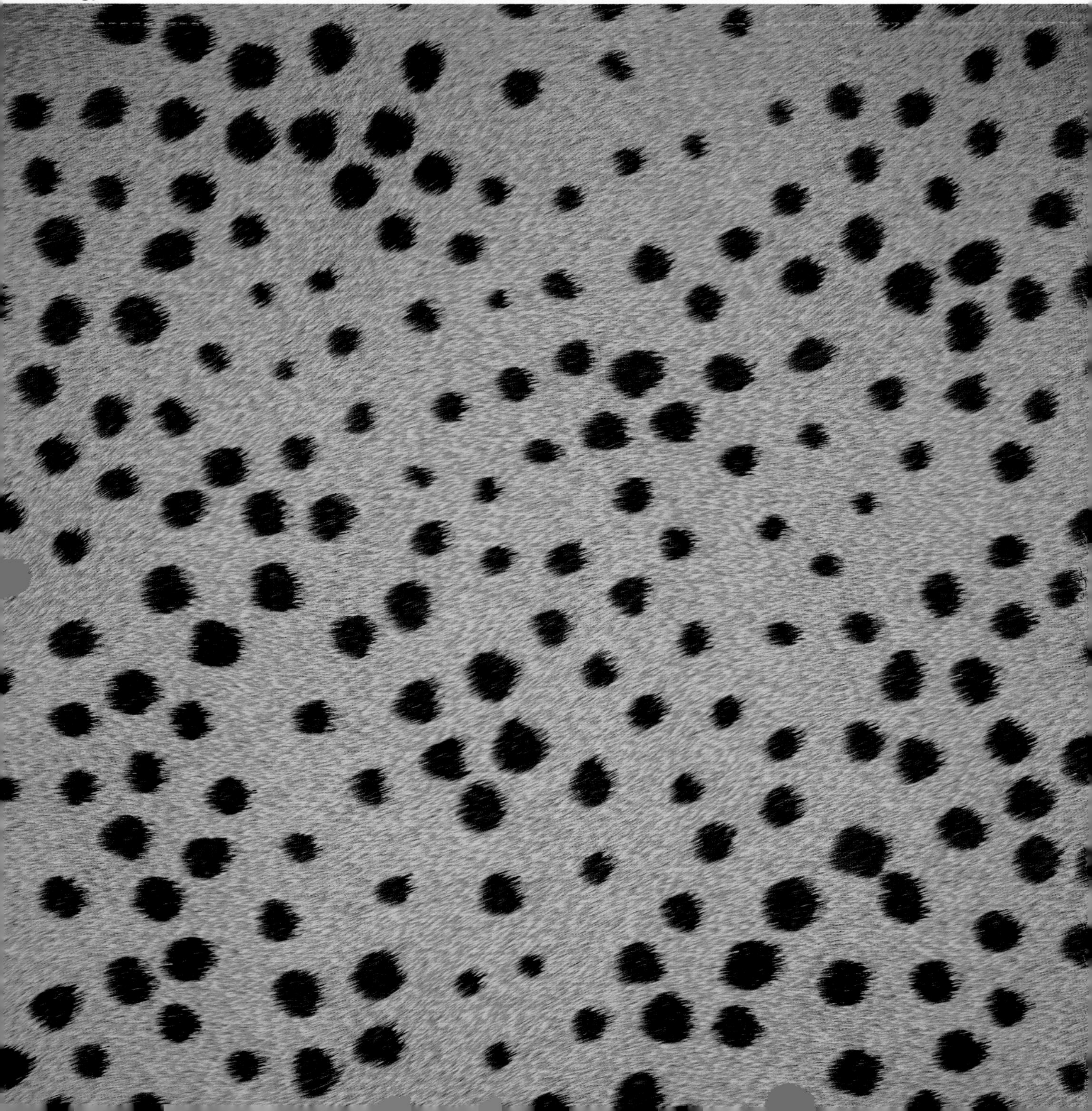

Recommended paper for the **Cat**: see diagrams and instructions on pp. 94–97

Recommended paper for the Leopard: see diagrams and instructions on pp. 94–97

Recommended paper for the Leopard: see diagrams and instructions on pp. 94–97

Recommended paper for the Leopard: see diagrams and instructions on pp. 94–97

Recommended paper for the Leopard: see diagrams and instructions on pp. 94–97

Recommended paper for the **Bulldog**: see diagrams and instructions on pp. 98–101

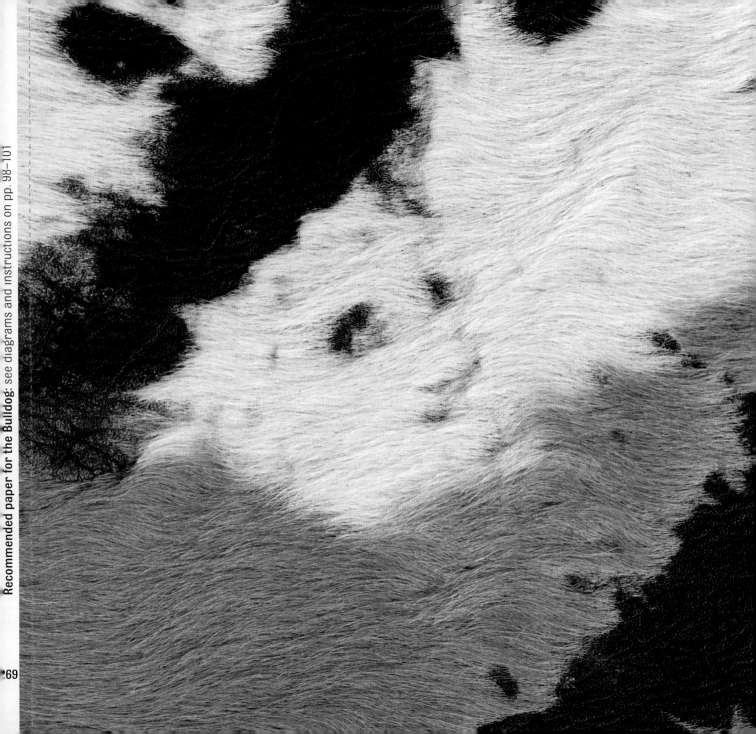

Recommended paper for the Bulldog: see diagrams and instructions on pp. 98–101

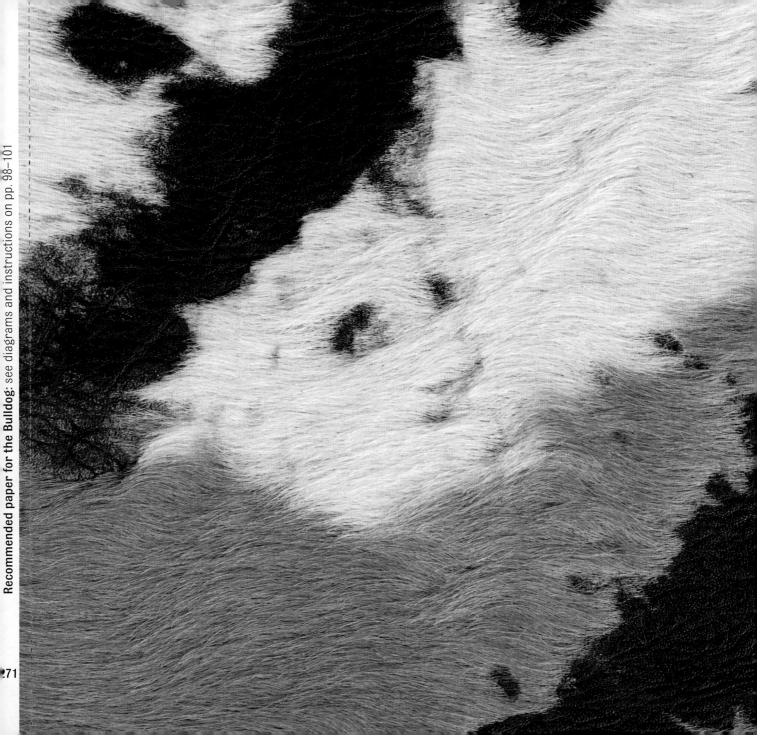

Recommended paper for the **Bulldog**: see diagrams and instructions on pp. 98–101

Recommended paper for the **Bear cub**: see diagrams and instructions on pp. 102–105

Recommended paper for the **Bear cub:** see diagrams and instructions on pp. 102–105

Recommended paper for the Bear cub: see diagrams and instructions on pp. 102–105

Recommended paper for the Bear cub: see diagrams and instructions on pp. 102–105

Recommended paper for the Three little rabbits: see diagrams and instructions on pp. 106–112

Recommended paper for the Three little rabbits: see diagrams and instructions on pp. 106–112

Recommended paper for the Three little rabbits: see diagrams and instructions on pp. 106–112

Recommended paper for the Three little rabbits: see diagrams and instructions on pp. 106–112

Recommended paper for the Three Little Rabbits: see diagrams and instructions on pp. 106–112

Recommended paper for the Three little rabbits: see diagrams and instructions on pp. 106–112

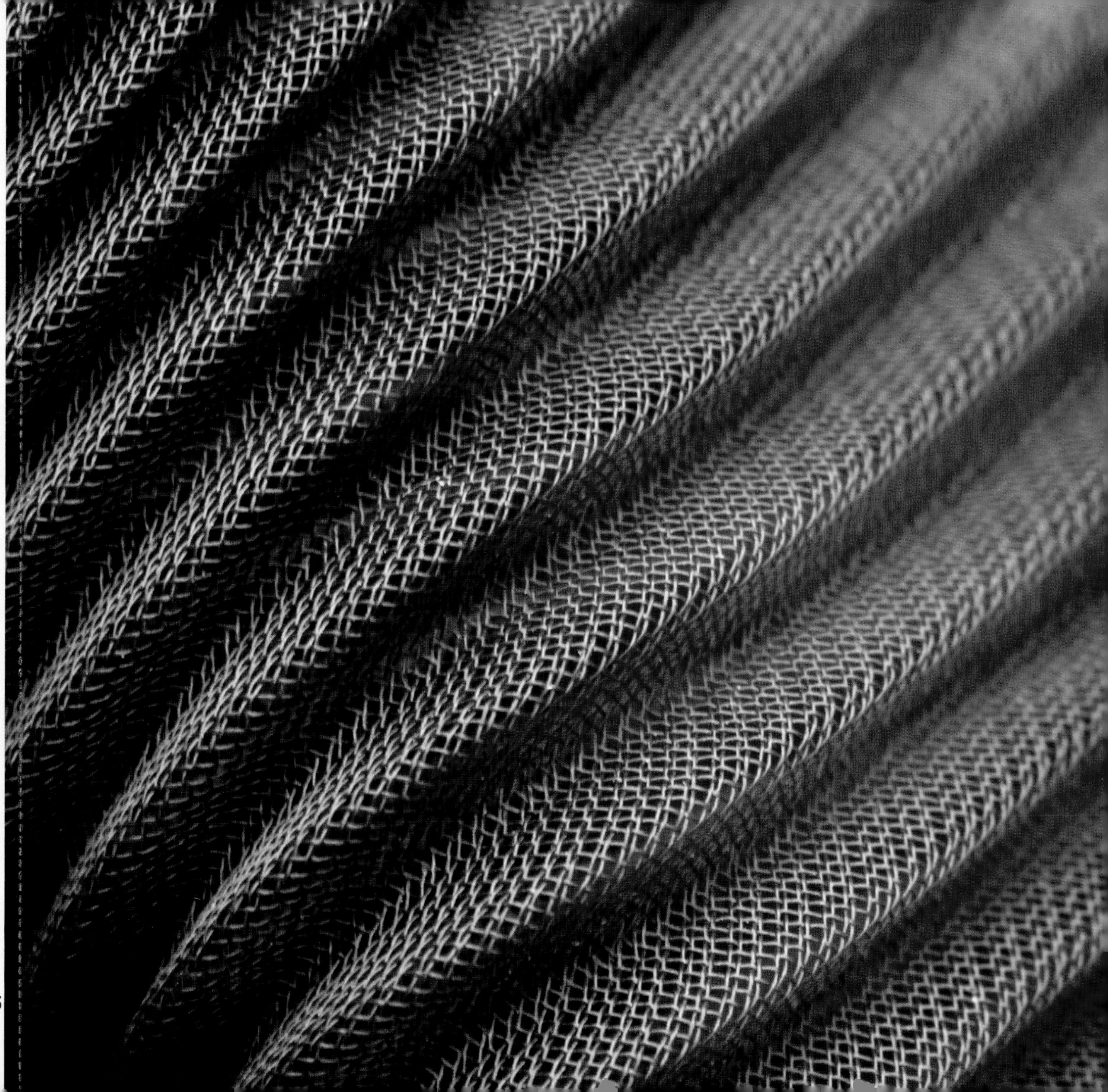

Recommended paper for the Three little rabbits: see diagrams and instructions on pp. 106–112

Recommended paper for the Three little rabbits: see diagrams and instructions on pp. 106–112

Recommended paper for the Three little rabbits: see diagrams and instructions on pp. 106–112

Recommended paper for the Three little rabbits: see diagrams and instructions on pp. 106–112

Recommended paper for the Three little rabbits: see diagrams and instructions on pp. 106–112

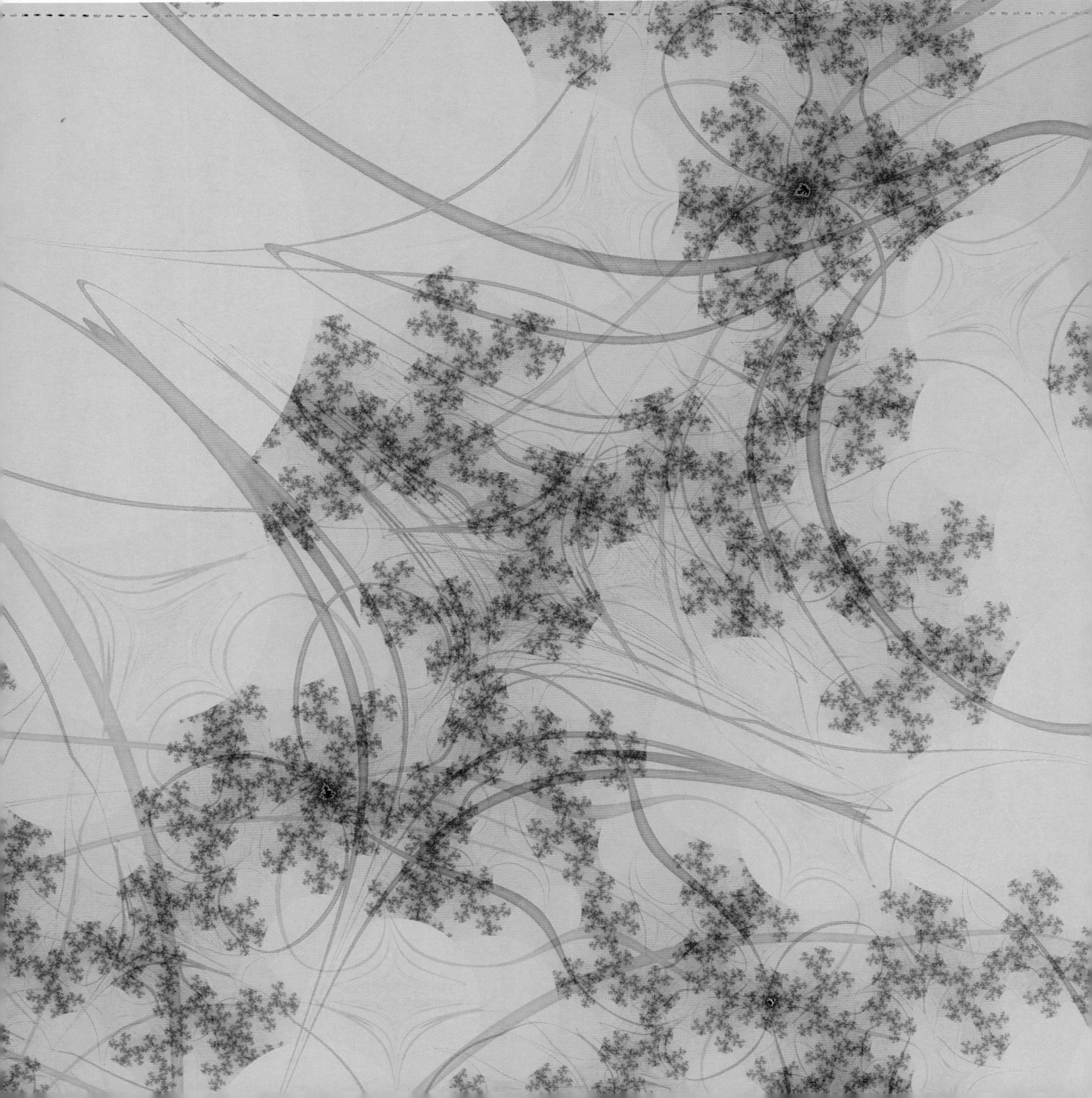

Recommended paper for the Three little rabbits: see diagrams and instructions on pp. 106–112

Recommended paper for the Three little rabbits: see diagrams and instructions on pp. 106–112

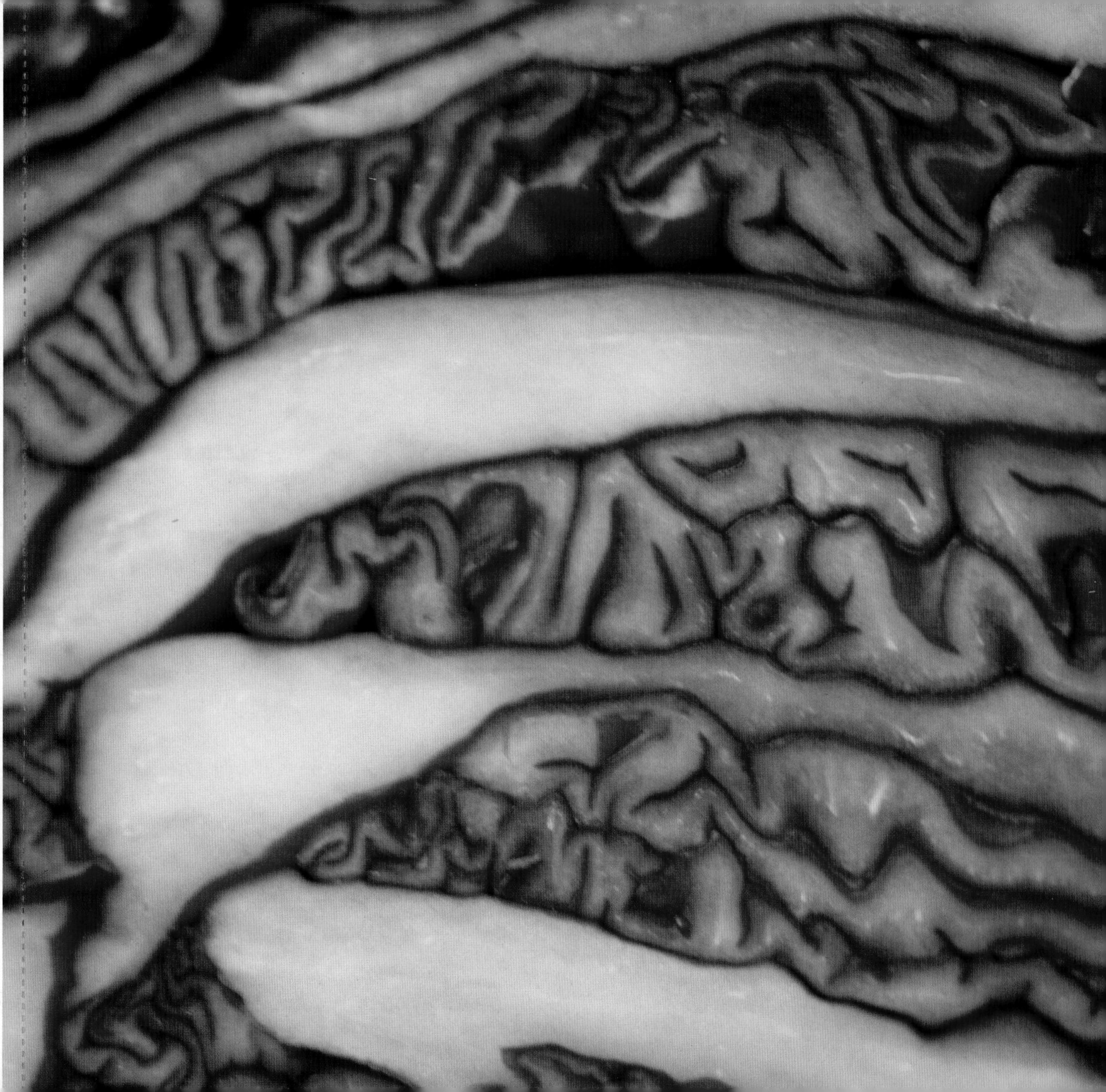

Recommended paper for the Three little rabbits: see diagrams and instructions on pp. 106–112

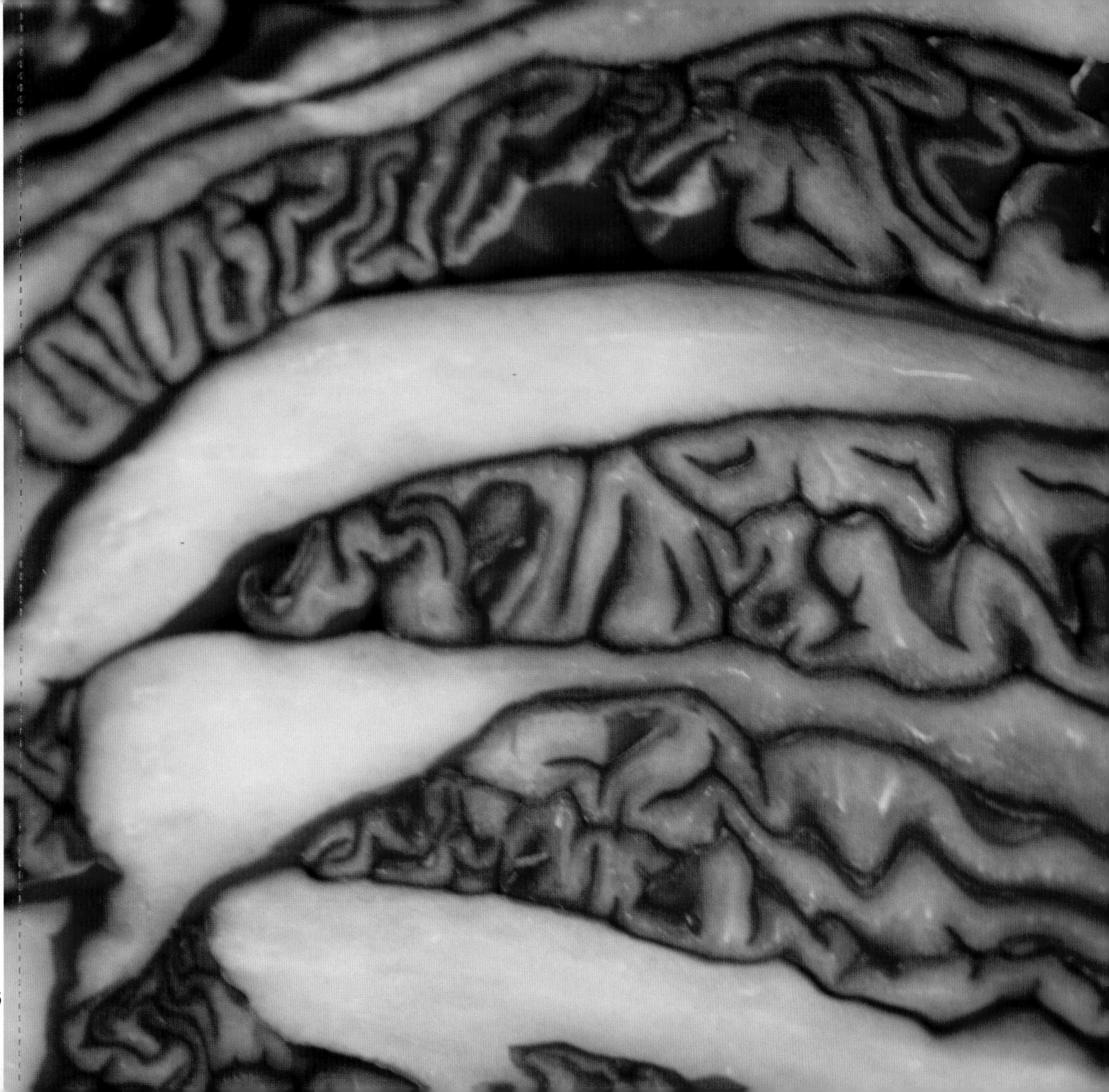

Recommended paper for the Three little rabbits: see diagrams and instructions on pp. 106–112

Recommended paper for the Three little rabbits: see diagrams and instructions on pp. 106–112

Recommended paper for the Three little rabbits: see diagrams and instructions on pp. 106–112

Recommended paper for the **Young cow**: see diagrams and instructions on pp. 113–116

Recommended paper for the Young cow: see diagrams and instructions on pp. 113–116

Recommended paper for the **Young cow** and the **Bull-calf**: see diagrams and instructions on pp. 113–116

Recommended paper for the **Young cow and the Bull-calf**: see diagrams and instructions on pp. 113–116

Recommended paper for the Bull-calf: see diagrams and instructions on pp. 113–116

Recommended paper for the **Bull-calf**: see diagrams and instructions on pp. 113–116

Extra paper so that you can let your imagination run riot...

Extra paper so that you can let your imagination run riot...

Extra paper so that you can let your imagination run riot...

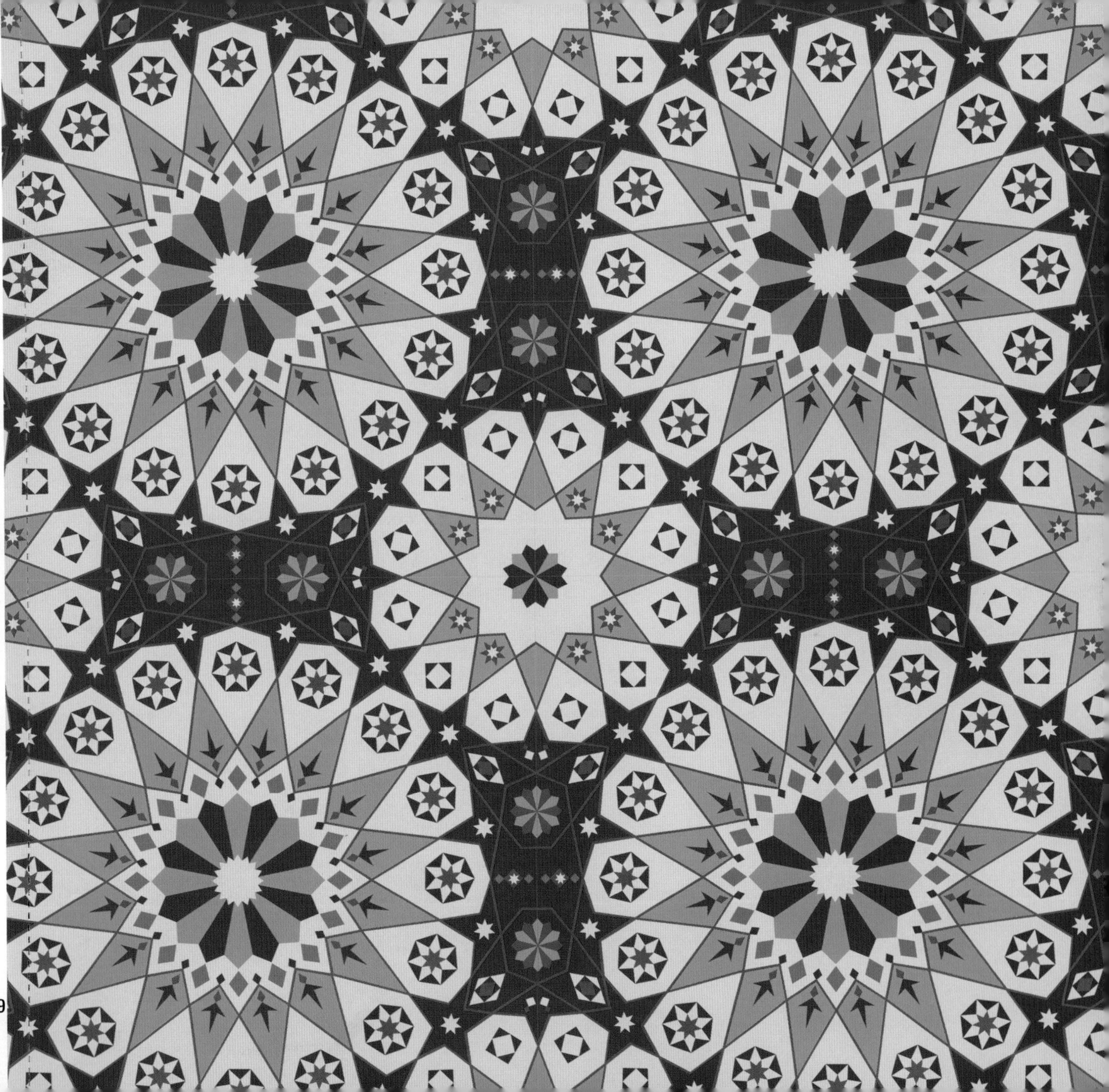

Extra paper so that you can let your imagination run riot...

Extra paper so that you can let your imagination run riot...